CAMBRIDGE LIBRARY COLLECTION

Books of enduring scholarly value

Religion

For centuries, scripture and theology were the focus of prodigious amounts of scholarship and publishing, dominated in the English-speaking world by the work of Protestant Christians. Enlightenment philosophy and science, anthropology, ethnology and the colonial experience all brought new perspectives, lively debates and heated controversies to the study of religion and its role in the world, many of which continue to this day. This series explores the editing and interpretation of religious texts, the history of religious ideas and institutions, and not least the encounter between religion and science.

The Present State of Ecclesiastical Architecture in England

Augustus Welby Pugin (1812–52), architect, writer, and designer, learned his draughtsmanship and love of medieval architecture from his father. Initially he was better known as a designer rather than an architect. His conversion to Roman Catholicism was a key moment for him, and shaped his subsequent career. His most famous book, *Contrasts*, was published in 1836, and expressed his belief in the aesthetic and moral superiority of pre-Reformation architecture. This 1843 book comprises two illustrated articles which had been published in the *Dublin Review* in 1841 and 1842, and examined recent English church buildings. During the 1840s there was a surge in church building, and bodies such as the Cambridge Camden Society hotly debated the connection between architecture and spirituality. In the first paper, Pugin discusses how to meet the needs of a small Catholic parish. In the second, he commends the influence of the *Ecclesiologist* on church architecture.

Cambridge University Press has long been a pioneer in the reissuing of out-of-print titles from its own backlist, producing digital reprints of books that are still sought after by scholars and students but could not be reprinted economically using traditional technology. The Cambridge Library Collection extends this activity to a wider range of books which are still of importance to researchers and professionals, either for the source material they contain, or as landmarks in the history of their academic discipline.

Drawing from the world-renowned collections in the Cambridge University Library and other partner libraries, and guided by the advice of experts in each subject area, Cambridge University Press is using state-of-the-art scanning machines in its own Printing House to capture the content of each book selected for inclusion. The files are processed to give a consistently clear, crisp image, and the books finished to the high quality standard for which the Press is recognised around the world. The latest print-on-demand technology ensures that the books will remain available indefinitely, and that orders for single or multiple copies can quickly be supplied.

The Cambridge Library Collection brings back to life books of enduring scholarly value (including out-of-copyright works originally issued by other publishers) across a wide range of disciplines in the humanities and social sciences and in science and technology.

The Present State
of Ecclesiastical
Architecture
in England

Augustus Welby Pugin

CAMBRIDGE
UNIVERSITY PRESS

CAMBRIDGE UNIVERSITY PRESS

Cambridge, New York, Melbourne, Madrid, Cape Town,
Singapore, São Paolo, Delhi, Mexico City

Published in the United States of America by Cambridge University Press, New York

www.cambridge.org
Information on this title: www.cambridge.org/9781108044837

© in this compilation Cambridge University Press 2012

This edition first published 1843
This digitally printed version 2012

ISBN 978-1-108-04483-7 Paperback

THE

PRESENT STATE

OF

ECCLESIASTICAL ARCHITECTURE

IN

ENGLAND.

BY

A. WELBY PUGIN, Architect.

WITH

Thirty-six Illustrations.

REPUBLISHED FROM THE DUBLIN REVIEW.

LONDON:

CHARLES DOLMAN, 61, NEW BOND STREET.

1843.

ECCLESIASTICAL ARCHITECTURE IN ENGLAND.

ARTICLE THE FIRST.

From the DUBLIN REVIEW, No. XX.
May 1841.

ECCLESIASTICAL ARCHITECTURE
IN ENGLAND.

ART. II.—*Elevation of the Cathedral Church of St. Chad, Birmingham.* By A. W. Pugin. London: 1840.

THE revival of our ancient parochial church architecture is a subject which occupies much attention at the present time; after three centuries of demolition and neglect, the solemn structures raised by our Catholic ancestors are being gradually restored to somewhat of their original appearance,* and buildings which but a few years since were considered as unsightly and barbarous erections of ignorant times, are now become the theme for general eulogy, and models for imitation. To the English Catholic there is no class of religious edifices of greater interest than the ancient parish churches of this country. They are admirably suited to the present wants and necessities of the Church, nor is it possible to adopt, consistently, any other models for the greater portion of our ecclesiastical buildings.

However glorious, magnificent, and edifying as were the great cathedral and abbatical churches, wonderful monuments of piety and zeal, we cannot turn to them in our present condition as objects of imitation. To rival them is wholly out of the question; to produce a meagre and reduced copy would be little better than caricaturing past glories. They were, in fact, the crowning result of Catholic piety and zeal, when it covered the face of the land, when all hearts and hands were united in the great work of rearing piles to God. These vast and sumptuous churches were, however, only the result of a long series of humble endeavours; they were the flowers of that faith which had been sown and cultivated by other means.

It is, in fact, by parish churches, that the faith of a nation is to be sustained and nourished; in them souls are engrafted to the Church by the waters of baptism; they are the tribunals of penance, and the seats of mercy and forgiveness. In them is the holy Eucharistic sacrifice continually offered up, and the sacred body of our Lord received by the faith-

---

* Among these restorations, none is more deserving of praise than that of the Temple church, London. The whole of the unsightly fittings of the last century have been removed, the marble caps and shafts beautifully restored, the whole of the vaulted ceiling diapered and painted, and many of the windows are being filled with stained glass, which, in design and execution, may vie with some of the richest windows of antiquity.

ful; there the holy books are read, and the people instructed; they become the seat and centre of every pious thought and deed; the pavement is studded with sepulchral memorials, and hundreds of departed faithful repose beneath the turf of the consecrated enclosures in which they stand. Each Catholic parish church is the history of the adjacent county; the family chantry, with its baronial monuments and heraldic bearings, the churchman's brass, the crusader's tomb, the peasant's cross, the storied windows, are all evidences of a long series of men and events; and valuable indeed are the national records furnished by many of even the humblest churches of this land; and even now, desecrated and despoiled as they are, still is there a traditionary reverence for these monuments of ancient piety left among the people.

Are not village spires, the church bells, the old porches, the venerable yew trees, the old grey towers, subjects on which writers and poets love to dwell? and Catholic feeling has never been so obscured in this land but that many have been found to view these holy spots with pious reverence; and what is truly consoling, the traditional form of the old buildings, although dreadfully debased and disfigured, has never been totally abandoned.* If the English Catholic body avail themselves of this feeling of attachment to the old parish churches which exists among a great body of the people, wonderful good may be produced; but if they neglect the means they are bound to employ to turn this feeling to the restoration of the old faith, then it will be found extremely inimical to the revival of religion.

A vast body of uninformed but excellently intentioned people, especially in agricultural districts, oppose the progress

---

* There are many interesting examples of this fact to be found in England. In that stronghold of Christian architecture, Oxford, we find colleges and buildings erected during the reigns of James and Charles, with the arrangement and features of the ancient buildings. At St. John's college are some beautiful groined ceilings of a very late date. The hall of Lambeth Palace, erected *since the restoration* by Archbishop Juxon, has buttresses, tracery windows, battlements, a lovre, a dais with a bay window, open framed roof, and all the characteristics of a refectory of the 15th century.

At Westminster Abbey the end of the north transept was almost rebuilt in the 17th century.

The font and cover at Durham Cathedral, set up in the time of Charles 1st, are carried up to a great height with niches, buttresses, and pinnacles.

The details of all these works are debased, and Italian monstrosities appear occasionally; but still these, and numberless other examples which might be adduced, fully prove that England long clung with a sort of lingering love to her ancient architecture.

of Catholicism from Catholic motives. They look upon the old church as the true one, they are not sufficiently instructed to draw a distinction between that same old church under Catholic or Protestant ministration, and they equally despise and avoid the dissenting conventicle, built by some independent preacher, or the *dissenting-looking* conventicle, erected in fact for the celebration of the very rites for which the old church was built, but with which it does not appear to have the slightest connexion, as an admirable writer in the *British Critic* beautifully expresses himself; " Grecian temple, Catholic cathedral, Corinthian portico, Norman doorway, pilaster and pinnacle, cannot differ so much or so essentially as the notions of a church, a preaching house, and a house of prayer. If then," he continues, "one could ensure the greatest technical accuracy in details, still if the Genevan principle of a house of God instead of the Catholic be adopted, the result must be an architectural monster." Such is the language of one, who, although unfortunately separated from us in communion, is evidently united in taste with the ancient faithful of this land ; and it is lamentable that few among us appear to feel the truth of these observations. Modern Catholics have frequently abandoned *Catholic architecture* for the *Genevan,* and even make light of this melancholy decay, and speak of the architecture of the house of God and the formation of his sanctuary, on which our Catholic ancestors bestowed the greater part of their lives and goods, as a thing indifferent, dependent on mere whim and idea. Now it is scarcely less important to adhere to the traditions of the Church as regards the arrangements of material buildings, than as to any other matters connected with the celebration of the divine mysteries; for it is impossible that these latter can be performed in accordance with the rituals and intentions of the Church, if the former are disregarded; and yet it is a melancholy fact, that even a great portion of the clergy seem utterly unconscious of the close connexion between the two.

The most ardent supporters of the modern temple or conventicle style, who have cast away without the least compunction, not only the splendours but the *proprieties and essentials* of church architecture, affect great horror of what they term innovation in matters of much less importance. They regard the reduction of a shovel-ended stole to its ancient and reasonable shape, or the unstarching of a crimped surplice and restoring its graceful and ample folds, in the light of an almost mortal sin; while they sever every link between themselves and Catholic practice and antiquity in the style and arrangement of their churches. Surely this must arise from want of due reflection or information on these matters.

Can it be imagined that the Church in all ages, would have defined with such scrupulous exactness every thing connected with the celebration of the divine office, had not such precautions been considered necessary to ensure a becoming and solemn performance of the sacred rites? The Church, moreover, appointed proper officers, such as archdeacons, and rural deans, to act under the bishop, and see that the intentions and regulations of the Church were properly carried out, and to report on the state of the various churches in the diocess.

There are yet existing visitations of the twelfth century, where the slightest defect or irregularity in the fabric or ornaments is carefully noted down, with directions for amendment; yet all these excellent regulations to preserve uniformity and discipline, established by the wisdom of the ancient Churchmen, are accounted as foolishness by many Catholics of these days. To assert the importance of adhering to ancient tradition in these matters, is sufficient to draw forth ridicule, and even censure. It is lamentable to hear the sentiments which are expressed on ecclesiastical architecture by many who should be most ardent in reviving it in all its ancient purity, but who do not even bestow as much consideration on it as on the construction of their stables. The principal part of our modern churches are the result of mere whim and caprice. Those who build them are regulated neither by ecclesiastical nor architectural authority; hence a new Catholic church is almost certain to be a perfect outrage on ecclesiastical propriety and architectural taste. It is impossible to say, before it is erected, whether the building will look most like an auction room or a methodist meeting; whether it will have any symbol of Christianity about it, or be quite plain; whether it will be a caricature of pointed or of Grecian architecture; whether it will have any characteristics of a Catholic church at all, if we except its extremely offensive appearance, which, grievous as it may be, is become a very distinguishing mark of a Catholic building.

Formerly, the word *church* implied a *particular sort of edifice invariably erected on the same principle ;* it might be highly ornamented, or it might be simple ; it might be large or small, lofty or low, costly or cheap, but it was arranged on a certain *regulated system.* *Churches built hundreds of miles apart, and with the difference of centuries in the period of their erection, would still exhibit a perfect similarity of purpose, and by their form and arrangement attest that the same faith had instigated their erections, and the same rites were performed within their walls.* But now, alas, the case is widely different; anything may be built and called a church; any style, any plan, any detail. No sooner is a new building of this kind determined upon, than there is a muster of committee-men to adjust preliminaries, and decide on plans. These are men generally ignorant of every thing connected with these matters; which the result of their labours but too plainly proves. Some Protestant builder,—a matter-of-fact one-idea Roman-cement man, whose highest achievement in architectural art has been the erection of a market-house, or modernizing the front of an hotel—is not uncommonly considered as a fit and proper person to design and carry out an edifice intended for those very rites which produced the erection of every truly fine church in the land. Of course this individual, who is perfectly destitute of any idea of what the church should be like, eagerly catches at the suggestions of the committee-men, who are far from backward in having a say on these occasions. One has seen a new chapel lately opened, which he thinks extremely *neat and pretty,* but would propose that the altar should stand in a sort of alcove; a second, however, objects to this latter proposition, as he proves that those who would sit in the *last seat of the gallery could not look down on the top of the altar;* this is declared to be a fatal objection, and the altar is decided to stand against a flat wall, where *it can be well seen on three sides.* A hints that something in the Gothic style would look well; but B declares it to be all *expensive gingerbread.* C, who has been to Rome, laughs outright at such a barbarism as pointed architecture, and asks A sarcastically if he ever saw a Grecian portico; talks with equally extravagant praise of St. Peter's and the Parthenon, the two most opposite buildings in the world, and concludes with an eulogium on classical taste and refinement, and the barbarisms of the old Catholics. A ventures to reply, that there was something very grand about the old churches, notwithstanding, and offering some remarks about antiquity, is cut short by a loud laugh and general cry, " Oh, we're *all for the modern now ;*" in which the one-idea Roman-cement man heartily joins, and compels him to be silent. After some further conversation about a marble altar from abroad, candlesticks of the newest Parisian fashion, and some other foreign novelties, the meeting separates, and a building is commenced, which in due time is finished, and opened with a band of theatricals, who, as the bills announce, have *kindly consented* to sing the praises of God—it might perhaps be added, as is sometimes seen on benefit bills, (*for that day only*), which would be an additional inducement for a full audience. This is a true picture of the manner in which many Catholic churches have been, and, what is worse, are still, being built; yet, perhaps, close by such an abortion stands the old parish church of the town. Although simple in its architecture, Catholic is indelibly stamped on its venerable exterior. Heretical violence has stripped it of its most beautiful ornaments; Protestant churchwardens have fattened on its old leaded roof and spire; it is curtailed of its fair proportions, and disfigured by some unsightly modern additions, which have been tacked on to its ancient walls; yet, in spite of these memorable disadvantages, it still tells its tale,—it is Catholic from foundation to tower top. Melancholy is it to think that this venerable pile should have been alienated from the ancient faith; but thrice melancholy is it that those who should ever regard it with veneration, and strive to imitate its beauties, should pass it by unheeded and despised; and as if in mockery of its venerable grandeur, raise a conventicle-looking structure under its very walls, where the assemblage of architectural monstrosities becomes a standing proof of the degeneracy of modern times.

It is very probable that many well-disposed persons have been led to approve, or at least tolerate, these miserable erections, from a mistaken idea that nothing could be accomplished in the pointed style under an immense cost. Now so far from this being the case, *this architecture has decidedly the advantage on the score of economy ;* it can be accommodated to *any materials, any dimensions,* and *any locality.* The erroneous opinions formed on this subject are consequent on the unfortunate results attending the labours of those who, when about to build in the pointed style, take some vast church for their model; and then, without a twentieth part of the space, or a hundredth part of the money, try to do something like it. This is certain to be a failure. Had they, on the contrary, gone and examined some edifice of antiquity, corresponding in *scale and intention to the one they wished to erect,* they would have produced a satisfactory building at a reasonable cost. Some persons seem to imagine that every pointed

church must be a cathedral or nothing: this has even been
cited as a reason why the proposed new Catholic church at
York should *not* be Gothic, on account of its vicinity to the
cathedral. Nothing can be more absurd: no one would think
for an instant of attempting to rival the extent or richness of
that glorious pile; but were there not above thirty parochial
churches anciently in York? and did their builders think it
expedient to depart from Catholic architecture in the design,
on account of the stupendous cathedral? Certainly not. There
were many buildings among them, and small ones too, *equally
perfect and beautiful for the purpose for which they were intended as the minster itself.* Architecture to be good must
be consistent. A parish church, to contain a few hundred
persons, must be very differently arranged from a metropolitan cathedral; and if this principle be understood, and acted
upon, the Catholics of York may erect an edifice suitable to
their present necessities, which would not be unworthy of
William de Melton or Walter Skirlaw

Churches must be regulated in their scale and decorations
(as was the case formerly) by the means and numbers of the
people; it being always remembered that the house of God
should be as good, as spacious, as ornamented, as circumstances will allow. Many a humble village church, of rubble
walls and thatched roof, has doubtless formed as acceptable an
offering to Almighty God (being the utmost the poor people
could accomplish) as the most sumptuous fabric erected by
their richer brethren. Everything is relative; a building may
be admirable and edifying in one place, which would be disgraceful in another. As long as the Catholic principle exists, of
dedicating the best to God, be that great or little, the intention
is the same, and the result always entails a blessing. But this
does not afford the slightest ground for a pretext, urged by
some wealthy persons in these days of decayed faith, that it
does not matter how or where God is worshipped, and that four
walls are equally well adapted for the purpose with the most
solemn piles. God expects, and it is beyond contradiction
His due, that we should devote to His honour and service a
large portion of the temporal benefits we enjoy. While, therefore, it would be both absurd and unjust to expect more than
what the station and means of persons enable them to contribute towards the erection of churches, it is a horrible
scandal, and a fearful condemnation, that many persons of
wealth and influence do oppose the Catholic principle, of
making the house of God the centre of earthly splendour; and

instead of contributing to this great and holy work, try to excuse their conduct by urging the miserable arguments of Protestants on these matters. While for the gratification of their own personal vanity, or the indulgence of their luxury, no expense can be too profuse, it is lamentable to look around on the various buildings used for Catholic worship in this land, and to see how few among them are at all fitted, either by their arrangement or decoration, for the sacred purposes for which they are intended.

We will not speak of chapels built fifty years ago, since it may with justice be urged that those were times of persecution; but we will turn to those churches which have been raised within a few years, and without the existence of any other restrictions than those which either the miserable parsimony or ignorance of the builders have imposed on them. In London itself, what are termed the *fashionable* chapels are uglier and more inconvenient than many Protestant chapels of ease; so ill-constructed as to arrangement, as to expose the sacred mysteries to unnecessary interruptions and publicity; so confined in their dimensions, that not a hundredth part of the people can squeeze in to hear mass; so meagre in decoration, that many Protestant churches are infinitely more elegant; and yet to these places, Sunday after Sunday, will Catholics of wealth, influence, and station, be driven in their carriages; and will appear, or actually are, perfectly satisfied with the building wherein they assemble to worship God, when the very entrance halls of their dwellings are more handsomely furnished, and the sideboards of their dining rooms are ten times more costly than the altar. In many country missions the case is even more deplorable; for we may find chapels destitute not only of the ornaments, but the essentials for the holy sacrifice, and even, horrible to name, the blessed Eucharist, the fountain of grace, received in a vessel of meaner material than what is generally used for the domestic table. The altar, composed only of a few boards, neglected, decayed, and dirty; candlesticks of the commonest description, holding an almost expiring wick; trash and trumpery, in the shape of paper pots of artificial flowers. are stuck about to make up a show, and the whole presents the chilling aspect of combined neglect, bad taste, and poverty.

But there is another sort of chapel, especially in large towns, which presents an equally offensive and distressing appearance, although from different causes; in these the evil does not proceed from either poverty or neglect, but from the ill-judged expenditure of money by pious but uninformed persons. In these places, societies of ladies are frequently formed for adorning the altar: the principal and ostensible object of such a sisterhood is admirable, but the manner in which the affair is carried out is generally lamentable. These well-meaning ladies transfer all the nicknackery of the work-room, the toilette-table, and the bazaar, to the altar of God. The result is pitiable ;—cut papers of various colours, pretty ribbons, china pots, darling little gimcracks, artificial flowers, all sorts of trumpery, are suffered to be intruded not only into the vicinity of the seat of most holy mysteries, but actually in the presence of the blessed sacrament itself, insulting to the majesty of religion and distracting to every well-regulated and informed mind. The pranks these well-intentioned but ill-judged devotees are allowed to practise are truly extraordinary. Their intentions are excellent; they wish to work for the good and advancement of religion, although they unknowingly hinder it, by rendering its externals childish and ridiculous in appearance. But why should not their efforts be turned into a good channel? let them embroider frontals of altars, which are susceptible of every variety of ornament and design; they should be varied for every festival, and have appropriate subjects and emblems worked on them for each. The orpheys and hoods of copes, and the crosses of chasubles, would be an ample field for the exertions of the most indefatigable needle-women; and beautiful church ornaments might they produce, if they would quit the Berlin pattern and pole-screen style, and imitate the ancient and appropriate embroidéry. We are greatly indebted to the ladies of the middle ages for much beautiful church needlework; but pure taste was then generally diffused, and *all worked in accordance with the regulations and traditions of the Church,* which were strictly enforced; and we may hope that such will again be the case, when Catholic art is better and more extensively understood.

But to return: there is another class of chapels, belonging to private mansions and families, which are generally in a most disgraceful state. Often has the butler a well-furnished pantry, the housekeeper her spacious storeroom, the cook his complete *batterie de cuisine,* all, in fact, well provided except the chapel and the chaplain: no pittance can be too small for the latter, nothing too mean or paltry for the former. There are some exceptions; but collectively they are quite unworthy of their sacred purpose; it would be invidious to name examples of either class, but we may mention some defects nearly common to them all, and leave the application of the remarks to those who may feel deserving of them.

The origin of these private chapels may be traced to both necessity and devotion. First: necessity, which during the times of persecution precluded the possibility of the public celebration of the Divine mysteries, and obliged the priests of the Church to seek privacy and concealment: hence the houses of those families who retained the ancient faith answered the purposes of parochial churches, and thus true religion was preserved by these means throughout the land. Secondly : the devotion of pious persons, who were anxious to have the consolations of religion under their very roof. Private chapels and chaplains are undoubtedly very ancient, and it is a practice which if properly carried out cannot be too much commended. It must be admitted, however, that it is a great privilege to have the same holy rites performed under one's own roof for which the most extensive piles in Christendom have been raised. The presence of the Lord of Hosts is no ordinary honour, and yet, strange to say, these reflections, if ever they are made, seem to produce but little effect on the minds of those who ought to be most sensibly touched by them. To *keep up a chapel* in these days is considered a *merit instead of a privilege;* a man is not accounted liberal who keeps a cook to administer to his appetite, a butler to provide him drink, and, in fine, a vast number of persons to attend and supply all he requires; this all passes by, nor is it of course considered any way meritorious; but to support a chaplain to administer the sacraments—without which all food, all raiment, all wealth, all state, is utterly dead and unprofitable— is thought in these days something very great and very praiseworthy. Out on such contradiction! the world does not in all its varieties exhibit such specimens of inconsistency as are to be found between the faith and practice of modern Catholics. If a visitor of fashion announces his intention of honouring their mansions with a visit, what preparations, what uncovering of holland, what setting up of wax lights; while the most holy sacrament of our Lord's body, deserted and forlorn, is left in a mean receptacle, without lamp or honour, in some half-furnished, half-dilapidated, and decayed chamber, which the owner of the house consents to give up to God, out of his vast and sumptuous residence; and while the commonest articles of food are served up on massive silver, by footmen in costly liveries, a miserable bit of plated ware is the earthly tabernacle for the sacred body of our Lord, and a cast-off gown is considered sufficiently good for a vestment wherein to offer up the adorable sacrifice. When a new private chapel is decided on, how often is some outhouse or adjacent stable converted into a sanctuary for the Lord of Hosts. Many private chapels have bed rooms *over* them, which is strictly forbidden ; others are situated directly over the meanest offices of the house ; and few indeed are there which have been arranged with the slightest reference to the sanctity of their purpose.

We cannot dismiss this part of our subject without referring to a chapel recently erected in the north, which is an instance much to be regretted of the foreign and novel ideas which exist among some of our most distinguished English Catholics. Money was lavished on this building with a zeal and devotion which would have done honour to days of livlier faith ; the endowment also was ample ; everything was done in a fine spirit, but with most mistaken ideas of Catholic architecture. A plaster imitation of Italian design has been erected on the soil of that county which can boast a Rivaulx, a Fountains, a Beverley, a York,—a county whose face is studded with Catholic remains of every style, from the severe lancet to the elaborate perpendicular. Alas ! Catholic England, how art thou fallen, when thine own children forget the land of their fathers, and leave thy most beauteous works unnoticed and despised, to catch at foreign ideas, unsuited to their country, and jarring with its national traditions.

The long exclusion of the English Catholics from the ancient ecclesiastical edifices, and the necessity which existed till lately of a foreign education, have undoubtedly produced this lamentable departure from the traditions and feelings of their ancestors. It is therefore of the highest importance to set forth the beauty and fitness of the ancient churches, and the necessity of adhering strictly to them as the models for our imitation. The majestic cathedral and celebrated ruin may occasionally arrest the attention of the modern Catholic traveller, but how few think on the interesting claims on their attention which *almost every rural church possesses!* how often do they pass unheeded the old grey tower and moss-covered chancel, when within their walls might be found many a memorial of old Catholic faith, which would not have survived the attacks of fanaticism and novelty in a more conspicuous spot. It is beyond even a doubt that the rural population of England were ardently attached to the faith of their fathers, and that but trifling changes were made in the internal decorations of the churches, till the ascendency of the Calvinists and fanatics under Cromwell; and even in the present day many of these ancient and holy edifices may be found tolerably perfect in their original internal arrangement.*

We will now consider what is to be regarded as forming a complete Catholic parish church for the due celebration of the divine office and administration of the sacraments, both as regards architectural arrangement and furniture. The building should consist of a nave, with a tower or belfry. A southern porch, in which a stoup for hallowed water should be provided; at the western end of the nave, and usually in the south aisle, a stone font with a wooden cover fastened with a lock, and near it an ambry in the wall for the oleum catechumenorum and holy chrism. The chancel at the eastern end should be separated from the nave by an open screen supporting the rood and rood loft, ascended by a staircase in the wall.

Wooden seats, with low backs, and placed wide enough apart to admit of kneeling easily, may be fixed in the nave and aisles, allowing alleys of sufficient width for the passage of processions. A stone or wooden pulpit sufficiently elevated may be erected in a convenient position in the nave.

The chancel floor should be raised at least one step above the nave, and the upper step on which the altar stands three steps above the floor of the chancel. The altar should consist of one slab of stone (marked with five crosses, and a cavity for relics) raised on solid masonry or stone pillars.

---

* Those churches which are situated in parishes too poor to admit of heavy rates, are invariably found in the best preservation. In wealthy towns, the parish churches have been considered as stock jobs, by which each ignorant shopkeeper, as he attains the office of warden, might enrich his pockets at the expense of the ancient fabric. In these buildings, the havoc which each trade has made in its turn may easily be traced. The carpenter has removed the carved and painted timbers of the roof, with the massive covering of lead, and set up a flat pitched slated covering in their stead, erected a few galleries, and *inclined planes* for seats; the painter has marbled and grained all the oak work left; while the glazier has carefully removed the stained windows, and replaced them by neat and uniform lights; the plasterer has stuccoed the chancel ceiling, and coloured down the stone work; the smith has lined the walls with stove piping, and set up a host of cast-iron furnaces; and each of these worthies is certain to record their achievements in some too legible inscription on the walls. St. Margaret's church, at Lynn, is a forcible illustration of this system. This magnificent fabric has been completely gutted of its ancient features. New roofs, new ceilings, new pavements, new pews, even plaster Italian ornaments stuck up to mask the old work. Immense sums have been expended to destroy every internal ornament and arrangement, simply on account of the *town being rich enough to bear the expense of these enormities;* for but a few miles from this very place are some most beautiful churches, secured by their poverty and neglect, where the carved angels yet enrich the oak-beamed roof, where the low-back sculptured benches yet remain; the fonts with their pinacled covers; the chancels divided off by the old traceried screens, on which the painted enrichments may still be descried, and so many of the ancient features left, that were it not for the unsightly reading-desks, and the decayed tables in place of the old and solemn altars, one would almost seem transported into some sacred edifice of the old time.

On the epistle side of the altar a sacrarium should be fixed, with a basin and waste pipe, with a stone shelf for the cruets. On the same side, and corresponding to the width of the three steps ascending to the altar, three niches should be built, partly in the thickness of the wall, and partly projecting, with canopies, and convenient seats for the priest, deacon, and sub-deacon. Opposite to these an arched tomb, to serve as the sepulchre for holy week. Adjoining the chancel, a sacristy or revestry for keeping the vestments and ornaments; or, in any small churches an almery may be provided for this purpose on the gospel side of the altar, within the chancel. An image of the saint in whose honour the church is dedicated, should be set up in the chancel. Where there are lateral aisles, they should be terminated towards the east by altars, either erected against the wall, and protected by open screen-work, or in chapels, eastward of the aisles, divided off from the church by screens. That these arrangements may be the better understood, we have subjoined four plans of Catholic churches now erecting in exact conformity with the ancient traditions.—(See Plates I, II, III, and below.)

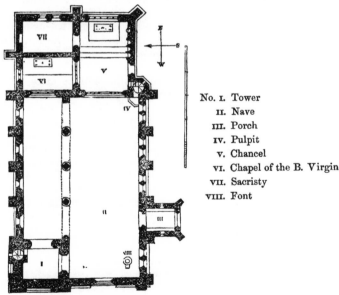

No. I. Tower
II. Nave
III. Porch
IV. Pulpit
V. Chancel
VI. Chapel of the B. Virgin
VII. Sacristy
VIII. Font

ST. MARY'S, STOCKTON ON TEES.

Having thus generally noticed the requisites for a church, we will now proceed to consider these in detail.

B

OF THE POSITION OF THE CHURCH.

A church should be so placed that the faithful face the east while at prayer. Such has been the practice of the Church from the earliest period, and very few are the examples of any deviation from this rule. The chancel should consequently be turned towards the east; and all the altars in the church should be so placed, that the celebrant, while officiating, looks towards the same quarter.*

Independent of all Christians turning towards the same point, being a beautiful figure of the unity of the Church, those learned writers, Durandus, Gavantus, and Cardinal Bona, have adduced the following reasons for this rule:—

1. That the apostles turned towards the east while at prayer.

2. That the Holy Spirit descended on them from the east on Pentecost.

3. That we should all turn towards the Holy Land, where our Lord was born.

4. That as our Lord was the great light of the world, we should turn towards the brightest quarter of the world, as a figure of his glory.

5. That as our Lord was crucified looking towards the west, the roods, placed in the same position, face the faithful.

6. That the star appeared in the east to the three wise men at the birth of our Lord.

7. To distinguish the faithful from infidels or heretics, who, being without faith or unity, turn in any direction.

8. That according to the traditional belief of the Church, our Lord will come from the east to judge the living and the dead.

But independent of these mystical and pious reasons, the ancient and canonical position is the most judicious that could have been chosen. How beautifully do the rays of the rising sun, streaming through the brilliant eastern windows of the choir or chancel, darting their warm and cheerful light to the very extremity of the nave, correspond to the hymn appointed to be sung at prime.

" Jam lucis orto sidere,
Deum precemur supplices,
Ut in diurnis actibus,
Nos servet a nocentibus."

---

* An inspection of a plan of an old cruciform church would readily shew how strictly this principle was adhered to in the arrangement of the various altars, whether in the transepts, extremities of aisles, or lateral chapels of apsics.

Then as the day advances, from the whole southern side a flood of light is poured into the building, gradually passing off towards evening, till all the glories of a setting sun immediately opposite the western window light up the nave with glowing tints, the rich effect being much increased by the partial obscurity of the choir end at the time.

Now this beautiful passage of light from sunrise to sunset, with all its striking and sublime effects, is utterly lost in a church placed in any other than the ancient position. In short, there are both mystical and natural reasons for adhering to antiquity in this practice, a departure from which can only be justified under the most urgent necessity.*

OF THE CHURCHYARD.

The inclosure within which a church was erected was set apart by solemn consecration for the burial of the faithful.†

And however objectionable places for interment may be in the midst of crowded cities, still it must be allowed that nothing can be more calculated to awaken solemn and devout feelings, than passing through the resting-place of the faithful departed. How often is the pious Christian moved to pray for his deceased brother, when he sees graven on his tomb,— " Of your charity pray for my soul"! What a train of profitable reflections, what holy meditations, may not be suggested by a sepulchral cross! In days of faith, prayer formed the link of communion between the living and the departed. Truly might it be said in time of old, when such pious respect was paid to the memorials and sepulture of the dead, " Oh, grave, where is thy victory! Oh, death, where is thy sting!"

Men formerly visited and knelt by tombs and graves; now they would shun them, and try and banish them from their sight as things odious and dreadful, and in accordance with the spirit of the times, which strives to make churches like

---

* We occasionally find examples of ancient churches, which, from the localities in which they have been erected, deviate from the usual position of west to east. These are, however, to be regarded as exceptions to the rule, and they can only serve as authorities for equally difficult scites.

† The first prayer in the beautiful office of the consecration of a cemetery is as follows :—

" Omnipotens Deus, qui es custos animarum et tutela salutis, et fides credentium, respice propitius ad nostræ servitutis officium, ut ad introitum nostrum purgetur bene+dicatur, sancti+ficetur, et conse+cretur hoc cœmeterium, ut humana corpora hic post vitæ cursum quiescentia, in magno judicii die simul cum felicibus animabus mereantur adipisci vitæ perennis gaudia. Per Christum Dominum nostrum. Amen."

assembly-rooms, gay and comfortable, with carriage drives and covered porticos to set down the company :—the very remembrance of death is to be excluded, lest the visitors to these places might be shocked at the sight of tombs.   Hence burying the dead is become a marketable matter, a joint-stock concern, an outlay of unemployed capital; and a large pleasure-ground, sufficiently distant from the town, is staked out by some speculators; in which, according to the prospectuses issued, every religion may have a separate parterre, with any class of temple, from the synagogue to the meeting-house.

However these sort of modern arrangements may suit the unitarian and the infidel, we hope and trust the Catholic church will still be surrounded by its consecrated inclosure, with its winding path, and its tombs, where the pious Christian may recite a *De Profundis* and a *requiem,* as he wends his way to the house of prayer, and still may the branches of the solemn yew tree* overshadow its arched porch.   It was customary to erect a stone cross, raised on steps, on the south-western side of the church to mark the hallowed ground ; and the shafts of these crosses, some of which were even Saxon, still remain in various churchyards, although the upper part has almost in every instance been destroyed by Protestant fanaticism. Wooden crosses, with the name of the deceased, and an invocation for prayer painted or cut on them, were erected over the graves of the faithful, in place of the hideous upright slabs, with bad poetry, pompous inscriptions, and ludicrous cherubs, now so much in vogue.   These sepulchral crosses are still set up on the Continent in villages, and such retired places as have yet remained in happy ignorance of urns, pedestals, broken pillars, and all the adopted Pagan emblems of mortality,† for which modern designers have abandoned the ancient and touching memorials of departed Christians.‡

---

* The branches of yew trees served anciently for palms in the procession of Palm Sunday.

† So blindly do artists of the present day adopt the ornaments and ideas of ancient paganism, that a stuff has recently been manufactured at Lyons intended for copes, to be used in funeral offices, in which the *poppy, emblem of eternal sleep,* has been introduced in lieu of those appropriate figures by which the joyful mystery of the resurrection (a Christian's brightest hope) was formerly represented.

‡ In an old English office-book belonging to the Scarisbrick family of Lancashire, the illuminated borders at the office for the dead are particularly curious. The whole of the ceremonies connected with a burial service are most accurately depicted.   The convoy, the hearse, and lights in the church, the celebration of the holy Eucharist, the recitation of the office, and the churchyard with the grave, are all introduced.   In this latter we have a perfect delineation of the

Besides these, some graves were covered with coped slabs, gradually diminishing at the lower end, with floreated crosses sculptured on them, and the inscription cut on each side of the stems ; and there are some instances of a later date, of regular altar tombs, with panelling and shields round them, having been erected in churchyards, of which there are examples at Glastonbury, Lavenham (Suffolk), and Bury St. Edmund's. Several of the Catholic churches now erecting will have cemeteries round them, disposed in the ancient manner, and from which all modern funeral monstrosities will be rigidly excluded.

OF THE EXTERNAL FORM AND DECORATION OF THE CHURCH.

The most striking and characteristic external feature of a church is its tower or spire. This is so attached to the popular notion of such a building, that any religious edifice wanting this essential mark would never generally receive any other appellation than that of chapel. Towers, attached to parochial churches, are most ancient in this country ; they appear to have been erected from a very early period, and several Saxon examples yet remain. It is a feature of ecclesiastical architecture which the establishment never abandoned even in its most degenerate period.

A church tower is a beacon to direct the faithful to the house of God ; it is a badge of ecclesiastical authority, and it is the place from whence the heralds of the solemnities of the church, the bells, send forth the summons. Let no one imagine that a tower is a superfluous expense,* it forms an essential part of the building, and should always be provided in the plan of a parochial church.

A tower to be complete, should be terminated by a spire : every tower during the finest periods of pointed architecture either was, or was intended to be, so finished ; a spire is in fact an ornamental covering to a tower ; a flat roof is contrary to every principle of the style, and it was not till the decline of the art that they were adopted. The vertical principle,

---

stone cross, the wooden crosses at the head of the graves, and all the interesting characteristics of an Anglo-Catholic parochial cemetery of the 15th century.

* If funds are not sufficient, the tower may be the last part of the building completed ; but due preparation should be made with regard to walls and foundations from the *beginning*, so that it may always be carried up when means will allow of its completion. This is the principle on which all the ancient churches were built. The *plan on which they were commenced was originally good*, and then they were gradually completed as the funds permitted.

emblematic of the resurrection, is a leading characteristic of Christian architecture, and this is nowhere so conspicuous or striking as in the majestic spires of the middle ages. The position of towers in parochial churches are various; they are generally placed at the west end of the nave, rising directly from the ground. This we will illustrate by three examples of Catholic churches now erecting;—the first is St. Giles's, Cheadle; the second the large parochial church of St. George's-in-the-fields; the third St. Oswald's, near Liverpool. —(See Plates IV, V, and VI.)

In cruciform parish churches, the tower is sometimes placed at the intersection of the nave and transepts, but of this we have no revived example at present.

We occasionally find the tower placed at the extremity of an aisle, and this expedient is usually resorted to in churches built in towns and confined situations, where there would not be sufficient space for a tower to project at the western end. Of this we give two examples;—the church of St. Wilfrid, now erecting at Hulme, near Manchester, and the church of St. Mary's, building at Stockton-on-Tees.—(See Plates VII and VIII.) To those whose ideas of architectural beauty are formed on the two and two system of modern building, this argument will appear very singular; but building for the sake of uniformity never entered into the ideas of the ancient designers; they regulated their plans and designs by localities and circumstances; they made them *essentially convenient and suitable to the required purpose, and decorated them afterwards.*

To this we owe all the picturesque effects of the old buildings: there is nothing artificial about them,—no deception,—nothing built up to make a show,—no sham doors and windows to keep up equal numbers,—their beauty is so striking because it is *natural.* The old builders did not think it necessary to build up a high wall to hide a roof, nor disguise a chimney into a flower pot; they made these essential parts of a building ornamental and beautiful: *this is the true spirit of pointed design, and until the present regular system of building both sides of a church exactly alike be broken up, no real good can be expected.* One of the greatest beauties of the ancient churches is this variety. It is impossible to see both sides of a building at once; how much more gratifying is it, therefore, to have two varied and beautiful elevations to examine, than to see the same thing repeated. A southern porch does not necessarily demand a northern one; a vestry on one side does not require an opposite one to keep up uniformity; a chantry chapel may be erected at the extremity of one aisle, without any necessity of raising up a building to look like it at the end of the other. A tower, if the locality require it, may be built on one side or corner of a church, without any obligation of building up another opposite.*

How many magnificent examples do we find among the ancient churches of towers placed in these positions, the entrances through them serving for southern porches. In very small churches, of exceedingly simple design, we occasionally find belfreys, in the form of perforated gables, or turretted projections, carved up at the end walls, and surmounted by

ST. MARY'S CHURCH, WARWICK BRIDGE.

stone crosses. These sort of belfreys are frequently found in ancient chapels, of which there is a beautiful instance yet remaining at Glastonbury. Among the revived Catholic buildings, some of the smallest have belfreys of this description, of which we give for examples,—St. Mary's on the Sands, Southport, Lancashire; St. Ann's, Keighley, Yorkshire,—(for which see Plate IX); and St. Mary's, Warwick Bridge, Cumberland.

It was usual to place a small belfrey of this description on the eastern gable of most parish churches; in which the Sanctus bell was rung to warn the faithful who might be in the vicinity of the church, that the holy mysteries were being celebrated. A very rich belfry for this purpose is to be placed on the east gable of St. Giles's church, now erecting at Cheadle.

---

* We are glad to perceive that the architect of the new Protestant church at Leeds has ventured to place his tower on the side of the building. This is certainly an advance towards better things.

OF THE PORCH.

The next part of the sacred edifice we have to consider is the porch. It was generally built to the southward, and in the second bay of the nave from the north end; there are several examples, however, of northern porches, and some few western ones, especially in situations much exposed to the wind of the sea coast.* Porches in England frequently consist of two stories, the upper room having been appropriated formerly to the purposes of a library, a school, or muniment room : occasionally these apartments appear to have been occupied by the sacristan, and they are sometimes provided with tracery apertures, through which the church would be watched at night.

Porches were, and ought now to be used for the following purposes :—

1. The insufflations of baptism were performed in the porch, where the child was exorcised previous to being admitted into the sacred building.

2. Women were churched in the porch after child-bearing.

3. The first part of the marriage service was performed in the porch.

4. Penitents assisted at mass in the porch during Lent.

Holy water stoups were generally hollowed out of the porch walls, and frequently built in niches on either side of the external arch, as at Bury St. Edmund's; all stoups for hallowed water should be placed *outside* the building. The custom of Christians sprinkling themselves with this water, is only a modification of the ancient custom of actually washing the hands and mouth, as an emblem of purification before prayer, which was generally practised in the early ages of the Church. It was for this purpose that large fountains and basins were placed near the entrance of great churches, many of which yet remain, as at St. Peter's at Rome, and several of the French cathedrals, Lyons, Chartres, &c. This custom among Christians is mentioned by St. John Chrysostom,† Eusebius, and

---

* At Cromer church, Norfolk, there are three magnificent porches, which have been suffered to go to shameful decay. At Cley church, Norfolk, there is a beautiful western porch ; also at Snetisham church in the same county. At King's Sutton church, Oxon, there is an elegant western porch of the early part of the 15th century, with effigies of the builders kneeling on each side of a niche, which anciently contained an image of the patron saint of the church.

† St. John Chrysostom in his " Homily on St. John,"—" Manus lavamus in ecclesiam ineuntes." The same in the Homily on St. Matthew"—" In ecclesia hunc morem obtinere cernimus apud multos, ut vestibus puris in templum ineant et ut manus lavent."

other writers of antiquity. Hallowed water was only taken on *entering* a church formerly, and never on leaving it. There is a regular ceremonial for presenting hallowed water to persons of distinction *on their entering* a church, but nothing of the kind was ever thought of on their departure. De Moleon, in his *Voyage Liturgique*, mentions several cathedral churches in France where the custom of taking holy water was strictly confined to entering. The original intention of this custom, which was to purify the soul *previous to commencing prayer*, having in a great measure been lost sight of, it is become usual to take the water on entering or leaving a church, indifferently. But Le Brun, who stands high as a writer on ecclesiastical or liturgical antiquities, thus speaks on this subject : " Those who are in the habit of taking hallowed water on leaving a church, are more moved to do so by the mere sight of the *bénitier* than by any consideration of the real intentions of the Church ; in this matter of which (he continues) the *curés de paroisse* neglect to instruct them."

Porches were frequently used as places of sepulture, even by persons of distinction. The great Talbot, Earl of Shrewsbury, directed his body to be buried in the porch of the parish church of Whitchurch.

From these remarks it will be seen that porches were not considered by our Catholic forefathers as mere places for scraping feet and rubbing shoes, but as a portion of the sacred edifice peculiarly devoted to the performance of solemn rites, and to be entered with due respect and reverence.

It may be proper to remark in this place, that the practice of selling books of devotion, rosaries, &c. in the porches of the churches, but too frequent on the Continent, is a great abuse ; such traffic is *strictly forbidden by the decrees of many synods and councils,* and those who tolerate the abuse are liable to severe ecclesiastical censures. That great champion of Catholic antiquity, Father Thiers,* who flourished during the

---

* The principal works of this great Theologian and learned Rubrician are as follows :—

1. "Dissertation sur les Autels."—2. " Dissertation sur les Jubés ;"—an admirable work, setting forth the antiquity and intention of roods and choir screens, and denouncing those innovators who ventured to remove them during the last century, and whom he most appropriately designates as Ambonoclasts.—3. "Dissertation sur le Clôture des Chœurs."—4. "Sur les Superstitions," in 4 vols. ; a most learned and laborious work, in which all the abuses which have existed at various times in the celebration of rites and ceremonies are separated from the decrees of the Church on those matters, and forms a most edifying and interesting exposition of true Catholic practices.—5. "Dissertation sur les Perukes," in

last century, openly denounced the chapter of Chartres cathedral for suffering two women to retail objects of devotion under the porches of that glorious church, which were intended for holy purposes; and at the time he published a most learned treatise on the use and intention of this portion of the church, and brought forward such overwhelming proofs of the irregularity of the practice, from the highest authorities, that the chapter, to their great mortification, were compelled to own their fault.

It cannot be urged in palliation of this great abuse, that the things sold are intended for holy purposes. The church has decreed that *nothing whatever shall be sold, either under the porches or within the edifice.* The dovesellers, whom our Lord cast out of the temple, traded only *in offerings;* and the profanation of the holy place is equally great by the traffic in candles, from which abuse so much scandal continually arises. We cannot, however, hope for any improvement in these respects from our foreign brethren, while they have so little feeling for the sanctity of the temple of God as to erect shoe stalls between the buttresses, and heap filth against the entrances, of the most glorious monuments of Christian antiquity. But we trust that the English Catholic churches will at least be preserved from these horrible profanations.

---

which the writer treats on all the coverings of the head used in the church, mitres, caps, callottes, amices; and also the antiquity of shaving the heads of persons devoted to the clerical state; on praying with the head uncovered, and the irregularity of ecclesiastics wearing wigs or false hair.—6. "Sur la Clôture des Religieuses."—7. "Sur les Porches des Eglises."—8. "Sur la Larme de Vendôme," a false relic formerly exposed at the church of Vendôme; a beautiful treatise on the Catholic doctrine touching the veneration of relics, and the abuses of the same.—9. "Sur l'Exposition du très Saint Sacrément;" in this work the discipline of the Church relative to the reservation and veneration of the blessed Eucharist, from the earliest ages down to the last century, is fully described, with the form and materials of the various vessels used for this sacred purpose; a work admirably calculated to set forth the sanctity and majesty of this most holy sacrament, and the antiquity of the Catholic doctrine touching the blessed Eucharist.—10. "Sur un Inscription dans une Eglise de Rheims en honneur de St. François;" a censure on an extravagant inscription set up by a Franciscan in a church at Rheims in honour of St. Francis (afterwards defaced by order of the archbishop), with an exposition of Catholic doctrine relative to the veneration and invocation of saints.

Those who are thoroughly acquainted with the works of this holy and learned writer, must be well instructed in ecclesiastical antiquity; for so great was his erudition and research, that he appears to have examined every source of information on this all-important subject. His works are now exceedingly scarce, for although approved of by the holy see, he was too sincere a writer, and fearless exposer of abuses for the corrupt age in which he lived. Acing on that grand principle expressed in these words,—" falsitas non debet tolerari sub velamine pietatis,"—he became one of the greatest witnesses of Catholic truth against the innovation of revived Paganism and Protestant error.

OF THE FONT.

On proceeding through the southern porch, and entering the church, the first object that arrests our attention is the font. Nor is its position so near the entrance without a sufficient reason. We have previously remarked that the exorcisms of baptism were performed in the porch; the priest then leads the catechumen, not yet regenerated by the waters of baptism, into the church, but far removed from the seat of the holy mysteries, the chancel; nor is he allowed *to approach the sanctuary till the all-important sacrament of baptism has been administered to him.* *

The font may be made either of stone or lead, sufficiently large to admit of immersion, with a wooden cover secured by a lock, to protect the baptismal water from any profanation. These covers were occasionally carried up with canopies and pinnacles to a great height, either suspended from the roof by a counterweight, or a portion of the tabernacle work made to open on the side. †

The new fonts at St. Mary's, Derby, St. Chad's, Birmingham, and Stafford, have covers of this description, surmounted by the appropriate emblem of a dove descending with rays. The font of St. Giles's, Cheadle, will stand within an enclosed baptistry at the western end of the south aisle, and will be furnished with a richly floreated canopy of the decorated period. When the importance of the holy sacrament of baptism, and necessity of administering it with becoming solemnity is considered, it would seem almost impossible that any Catholic church should be unprovided with a regular font. It is a lamentable fact, however, that this most essential piece of church furniture is seldom to be found in modern Catholic churches,—a jug and basin, such as might be used by puritans and fanatics, being often the only substitute, and these in places where silver tea services are being subscribed for the clergyman. But the poorest church should be provided with a regular stone font, and as it is possible to erect one under £10, the expense cannot be an obstacle to their general

---

* How often in these days of decayed discipline is the whole baptismal service performed within the sanctuary, destroying all the mystical illusions of the ancient arrangement, and admitting a soul under the curse of original sin, at once into the holy of holies. This, among other departures from ancient usages, has arisen in a great measure from the impracticability of following ancient rites in the modern conventicles built for Catholic worship.

† At Sudbury church, Suffolk, Selby church, Lincolnshire, Fosdyke church, Lincolnshire, and St. Peter's, Norwich, are fine examples of canopied covered fonts. The latter is peculiarly beautiful in its design.

restoration. Each of the churches engraved in this article is provided with fonts, canonically placed, corresponding in style and ornament to that of the building, and for the most part these churches have been completed for considerably less sums than the plastered and cemented assembly-rooms raised for Catholic worship in later times, which are deficient in every requisite for the sacred purpose for which they have been erected.

OF THE NAVE AND AISLES.

These form the portion of the edifice in which the faithful assist during the celebration of the holy mysteries. Nave is undoubtedly derived from the word *navis*, or ship, a figure often used with reference to the church. Aisle is derived from the French, and signifies wing or side, and can be only applied with propriety to the lateral portions of the building. Middle aisle is a contradiction of terms; side aisle becomes tautology. In the ancient arrangement of the faithful, the men were placed in the upper part of the nave, and the women behind at the lower end; but, by the custom of later times, the women were placed on the gospel side, and the men on the epistle. The appropriation of particular seats and distinction of places was strictly forbidden among the two classes.* Seats were used in the *parochial* churches in England from a very early period, and many of these remain tolerably perfect at the present time. They were very low, and wide apart, for the greater convenience of kneeling, open at both ends, and sometimes most beautifully ornamented with carving.† The pulpit should be placed in some convenient part of the nave, either against a pillar, or by the chancel arch. The ancient churches were generally provided with a pulpit of wood or stone, many fine examples of which are yet to be

---

* By a decree of the synod of the diocese of Exeter in 1284, no one should claim any seat in a church ; but whoever first entered a church for the purpose devotion, might choose at his pleasure a place for praying.

† At Little Walsingham church, Norfolk, the whole of the ancient seats remain quite perfect ; the backs are enriched with perforated tracery of varied design, and the ends are carried up into foliated finials.

On the seats of Warksworth church, Oxon, the creed is carved in a string course round the backs, and on the ends a representation of the Annunciation of our blessed Lady, and other mysteries, with the pious donor of the seats represented kneeling at prayer, with a scroll and a scripture.

The lords of the manor had occasionally a sort of pew, like a chantry chapel, of which there is a fine example at Lavenham church, Suffolk, and the patron of the church was usually permitted to sit within the chancel ; but both these customs may be considered as departures from pure discipline.

found. It is to be remarked that the pulpits were far different from the cumbrous rostrums used for the purpose in the present day, and we need hardly observe that the monstrosity of a reading-desk is a pure Protestant introduction. In the view of the nave of Southport church, as well as Cheadle, it will be seen that the pulpits are fashioned precisely on the old models, corbeled out, and ascended by the rood stairs, and not so large as to form a prominent feature.

At the eastern end of the nave, over the great chancel arch, the Doom or Last Judgment was usually depicted. The reason for placing this awful and certain event so conspicuously before the people is too obvious to need any comment. Most of these edifying paintings were defaced, under Edward the Sixth, as superstitious, but one has been newly discovered at Coventry, which, although very late and coarse in execution, is exceedingly curious.

At the eastern end of the aisles should be small altars; that on the southern side was usually dedicated in honour of our blessed Lady.* These altars should be protected by open screens enclosing chapels, called percloses. There are many remains of such screens and enclosures in old parish churches, but the altars have been invariably destroyed.

OF THE CHANCEL SCREEN, ROOD, AND ROOD LOFT.†

From the earliest ages there has been a separation between priest and people, between the sacrifice and the worshippers, in every church. They have been various in materials, in construction, and in arrangement, but have always existed in some form or other.‡ In parish churches, these screens were generally built of wood, and consisted of open tracery panels,

---

* It may be proper in this place to notice a very common error, of speaking of churches and altars as being dedicated *to* such a saint. The Church has never sanctioned the dedication of a church *to any* saint; they *are all dedicated to God*, (but according to a most ancient and laudable custom), *in honour* of certain saints, by whose names they are distinguished.

† It is worthy of remark that the first rood erected in England since their destruction by act of Parliament, was set up in the private chapel of Ambrose Lisle Phillipps, Esq. of Grace Dieu Manor, a zealous restorer of Anglo-Catholic antiquity. In this chapel most solemn service is performed on Sundays and festivals, the Gradual chaunted from the Lettern, and the whole office sung by men and choristers in the devotional and sublime plain chant, the only music sanctioned by the Church.

‡ In a continuation of this article, it is proposed to enter fully into the history of rood lofts, when describing the arrangements of cathedral and conventual churches, where they were used for more solemn purposes than in the parochial ones.

from about three feet from the floor, with an entrance capable of being closed by doors with open panels; their height varies from eight to fifteen feet, according to the scale of the church, and their breadth extends the whole width of the chancel arch, or in a choir church the breadth of the nave.* The carving on many of these screens is most varied and elaborate, and independent of the important mystical reasons for their erection, they form one of the most beautiful features of the ancient churches, and impart much additional effect to the chancel when seen through them. Like other parts of the interior, these screens were enriched with painting and gilding, and on the lower panels it was customary to figure saints and martyrs on diapered grounds.†

THE ROOD LOFT

Was a gallery partly resting on the screen, and running across the whole of its width, frequently supported on arched canopied work rising from the screen. The ascent to these lofts in large churches was usually by two staircases; but in small parish churches one was considered sufficient. It was carried up either in the pier of the chancel arch, or in a small turret outside the wall, and communicated with the rood loft by a narrow gallery, of which there are several examples at Stamford. We will not refer in this place to the use of these rood lofts or *jubés* in large buildings, but confine our remarks to their purpose in parochial churches.

Their first and most important use was to serve as an elevated place from whence the holy Gospel might be sung to the people, according to a most ancient and universal practice of the Church, of singing the holy Gospel from a raised place.‡

---

* Many of the large parish churches had regular choirs with stalls, as at St. Peter's, Norwich; St. Mary's, Coventry; Long Melford church, Suffolk. In these churches there were no arched divisions between the nave and choir, the separations consisted only in the screen and rood loft over it.

† It is not unusual for modern artists to decry the ancient system of decorating churches with much painting; but those who raise these objections seem to forget that what is technically termed keeping, is quite as requisite *in a building* as *in a picture*. The moment colour is introduced in the windows, the rest of the ornaments must correspond,—the ceiling, the floor, all must bear their part in the general effect. A stained window in a white church is a mere spot, which, by its richness, serves only to exhibit in a more striking manner the poverty of the rest of the building.

In the old churches, the azure and gilt ceiling, the encrusted tiles of various colours, the frescoes on the walls, the heraldic charges, the costly hangings of the altars, the variegated glass, all harmonized together, and formed a splendid whole, which can only be produced by the combined effect of all these details;—omit any of them, and the unity of the design is destroyed.

‡ The ambones of the ancient Basilicas served for this purpose.

2. The whole of the Passion of our Lord was sung from the rood loft;* the Gradual and other parts of the mass were chanted, and small organs fixed on the rood loft.

3. Lessons were read from the rood loft in many churches, and holy days announced to the people.

4. On great feasts, lights were set up in the rood loft, and at Christmas and Whitsuntide it was decorated with boughs and evergreens. Immediately in the centre of the loft stood the rood or cross, with an image of our Lord crucified, and on either side the blessed Virgin and St. John. The cross was usually floreated,† and terminated at the extremities with quatrefoils, and emblems of the four evangelists; on the reverse of which the four doctors of the Church were not unfrequently carved.

To illustrate these screens and roods, we have figured various churches, either completed or in course of erection.

The first is the interior of St. Mary's, Southport,‡ (see Pl. X)

---

* "There was a fair rood loft, with the rood, Mary and John of every side, and with a fair pair of organs standing thereby; which loft extended all the breadth of the church. And on Good Friday, a priest there standing by the rood sang the Passion."—*Records of Long Melford Church.*

† It is worthy of remark, that the ancient crosses were all richly decorated, in order to set forth that the very instrument on which our divine Redeemer suffered an ignominious death had become the emblem of his glorious victory over sin and its punishment, and should therefore be ornamented as the figure of this great triumph and our redemption. The old mystical school of Christian painters invariably figure our Lord with *extended* arms on the cross,—not through ignorance of drawing, but to represent the Son of God embracing the sins of the whole world. Not unfrequently, too, do we find the figure of the blessed Virgin and St. John much smaller in proportion than that of our Lord. This was done solely for the purpose of expressing the majesty of God. If we only examine attentively the productions of the ages of faith, we shall find that they convey a profound mystical meaning; and many conventional modes of representing the sacred things, that have been described by modern upstarts as proofs of barbarous ignorance, are in fact the most convincing proofs of the piety and wisdom of those who produced them. Their productions are addressed to the *understanding*, not merely *to the eye*, and there is more edification to be gained from a Saxon cross, with its enamelled emblems, than in all the anatomical crucifixions of modern times, in which the whole efforts of the artists appear to have been directed towards producing a distorted representation of a dying malefactor, instead of the overpowering sacrifice of the Son of God. It *is much safer to treat those holy mysteries in a conventional and emblematic manner, than to aim at unattainable realities.* The celebrated Crucifixion of Rubens is painful, not to say disgusting; certainly not edifying. The Christian artists have enveloped every incident of our Lord's life and suffering with a spiritual and mystical form, calculated to impress the mind with deep veneration for the sacred truths they represent. Sooner or later Christian art will be appreciated as it deserves, and the semipagan representations of the last three centuries, (in which *sacred things have only been made a vehicle to exhibit the lascivious art of modern painters,* who scrupled not, when professing to embody the blessed Virgin herself, to select their models from the profligate and abandoned) will sink into the abhorrence they deserve.

‡ This building, which possesses every requisite for a parochial church,—

of which an exterior prospect is given on Plate IX. This church being exceedingly small, the chancel screen is merely surmounted by the rood without any loft; the screen as well as the cross are diapered and painted from ancient examples. The second is the name of St. Alban's church at Macclesfield, just completed. (See Pl. XI.) Here is a regular rood loft, ascended from a staircase in the southern chapel, twelve feet from the chancel floor, surmounted by a cross, with the usual accompaniments. The images of this rood are of ancient German work of the 15th century, and were removed from their original position during the invasion of the French.

The eastern window seen through the screen, is filled with rich stained glass, given by John the present Earl of Shrewsbury, a great benefactor to this church. In the tracery are angels, habited in albs, bearing scrolls with various scriptures, and shields with emblems of our Lord's passion; the Talbot lion is also introduced in the quatrefoils.

In the centre light is an image of St. Alban, protomartyr of England, standing under a canopy; the other lights are filled with quarried glass interspersed with emblems.

The sedilia and dossell of altar are of stone; this latter consists of a row of canopied niches, richly carved and filled with images of apostles.

On either side of the screen hang two damask curtains of crimson, and a frontal is suspended before the altar. At the end of the southern aisle is a chapel dedicated in honour of our blessed Lady, and divided off by an open screen in a stone arch. The church is capable' accommodating from eight hundred to one thousand persons, and its total cost, with the tower complete, will be about 6000*l*.

The third example is a transverse section of the great church now erecting in St. George's Fields, London (see Pl. XII), shewing the great rood screen and loft,* with the screens and chapels terminating the aisles. The width of the nave is 28 feet, the aisles 18 feet; and the length, exclusive of chancel and tower, 160 feet; the chancel will be 43 feet in depth, with stalls on either side, and the side chapel 20. The great chancel window will be filled with the genealogy of our Lord, on the root of Jesse, in rich stained glass, the gift of

---

nave, chancel, rood and screen, stone altar, sedilia, sacrarium, southern porch, stoups for hallowed water, font and cover, bell, turret, organ and loft, open seats, stone pulpit, stained glass, and is capable of holding 300 persons,—has been erected for 1500*l.*, including every expense.

* This rood loft is ascended by two staircases, which will be seen by reference to the plan. These staircases terminate outside in pinnacled turrets.

the Earl of Shrewsbury; and every detail of the building will be carried out in the style of the time of Edward III. A great part of the church will be left open, without seats, and three thousand persons may be easily accommodated on the floor. No galleries of any description will be introduced, but all the internal arrangements will be strictly a revival of those which were anciently to be found in the large parochial churches of England.

The fourth example is a section of a small, simple, but complete church, lately erected at Dudley,* (see Pl. VII)

---

* This church, which is calculated to hold six hundred parishioners in the nave and aisles, stands on a declivity on the south-east side of the castle. The sacred edifice is surrounded by a cemetery, in which a stone cross is erected, and at the western extremity of the land a small simple parsonage house is now erecting, to which will be added a school.

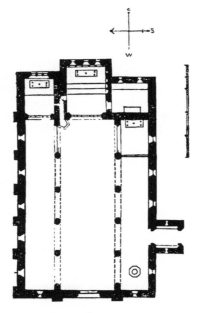

ST. MARY'S, DUDLEY.

The references of the plan will shew that this church possesses every canonical requisite for its sacred purpose. The eastern windows are filled with stained glass of a mosaic pattern, interspersed with emblems and subjects: in the chancel are ancient images of our blessed Lady and St. Thomas of Canterbury; while the vestry is furnished with a complete set of sacred vessels and ornaments, of which the following is an inventory:—a processional cross, wit Mary and John; a

C

which will be dedicated in honour of our blessed Lady and that glorious martyr St. Thomas of Canterbury.

The fifth example is a view of the interior of St. Giles's, Cheadle, now erecting, (see Pl. XIII.) Over the great chancel arch will be seen the Doom painted on the wall; at the eastern end of the aisles are screens inclosing chapels with altars; the pulpit is placed on the gospel side of the chancel arch; the rood loft is supported by arched ribs over the screen, and is ascended by the staircase which leads to the pulpit.

This church, which is being raised at the sole charge of the Earl of Shrewsbury, will be a perfect revival of an English parish church of the time of Edward I; decidedly the best period of pointed architecture. The floor will be entirely laid with encrusted tiles; every window will be filled with painted glass; and the smallest ornaments will be finished with scrupulous regard to correctness of style. We refer the reader to the plan, and west elevation of this church, at Plates I & IV; also to the engraving of the chancel, at Plate XVI.

OF THE CHANCEL.

We now come to the place of sacrifice, the most sacred part of the edifice; and well may we exclaim, when passing beneath the image of our Redeemer, and through the separating screen of mystic import, into this holy place, " O quam terribile est locus iste." The ancient chancels were truly solemn and impressive, and those who have souls to appreciate the intentions of the old Catholic builders, must be edified with their wisdom and propriety, in keeping the seat of the holy mysteries at a reverential distance from the people, and in setting forth the dignity and privilege of the priestly office, by separating the ministers who are offering up the holy sacrifice from the worshippers. " Cancellos qui circumstant altaria presbyteri tantum et clerici ingrediantur: neque ullo modo ibi seculares maxime dum divina mysteria celebrantur admitti debent," says Merati in his Commentaries on Gavantius;

---

holy water vat and asperge for processions; a silver gilt chalice, with an enamelled foot of the thirteenth century; a ditto ciborium, with an ancient foot; a pair of cruets; a copper gilt thurible; a pair of triple candlesticks, for the high altar; a pair of small ditto, for chapel of blessed Virgin; a small tower, for the reservation of the blessed sacrament; a basin and pricket, for a light for the high altar; a set of vestments, of each colour; an apparelled alb and a plain alb; a frontal for the high altar; a ditto of velvet and gold embroidery, for the altar of Lady chapel; a set of altar cloths; corporal cases; an ornamented cross, for the altar. The whole cost of this building, including all the abovementioned ornaments, vestments, stained glass, architect's charges, and every expense, was 3165*l.*; which fully proves for how moderate a sum a real Catholic church may be erected, if the funds are judiciously employed.

and if the mysteries of religion are to be held in reverence by the people, the old traditions and observances must be restored and enforced. Of all lamentable innovations, the wretched recesses substituted for chancels in modern churches are the most horrible : the altars are not only crowded up by seats, but *actually overlooked,* and the sanctity of the sacrifice itself partially disregarded. If these barriers round the holy place were considered necessary in days of faith, how doubly are they wanted at the present time! Churches are now built on exactly the same principle as theatres, to hold the greatest number of persons in the smallest possible space ; and the only difference in the arrangement is the substitution of an altar and altarpiece for the proscenium and drop-scene. What is the consequence? Catholic feeling is soon lost among the people : there is not even a corner for holy meditation or retired reflection ; they are filled and emptied like dissenting meeting-houses. The worshipper is either in a mob, or in the odious and Protestant distinction of a private pew. The humblest old Catholic church, mutilated as it may have been, is ten times more impressive than these staring assembly-rooms, which some persons, in these days, consider the most appropriate erections for Catholic worship.

The first view of a chancel is that of St. Wilfred's church, now erecting at Hulme, near Manchester.* (See Pl. XIV.) Here the altar is of a very early form, the front being open, and the top slab supported by stone pillars, three in number, gilt and painted. Under the altar is deposited a shrine† with relics, round which a velvet curtain is occasionally drawn.‡

---

* This church, as may be seen on reference to the plan, (Pl. III) consists of a nave and two aisles, with a tower at north-western corner. Eight hundred persons may be seated in the body of the church, besides a considerable open space left at the lower end. The eastern chapels are divided off, by open screens, from the aisles, and also from the side arches of chancel. The font is placed near the southern porch. At the south-eastern end is the sacristy, communicating from the chapel of the blessed Virgin, and fitted up with almeries and all requisite fittings. Attached to the church, by a small cloister, is a large and commodious parsonage house for the residence of the clergy. The church, house, enclosure of ground, and all internal fittings, as well as every essential ornament for divine service, also architect's commission, will not exceed the cost of £5000.

+ Shrines were very frequently placed under the ancient altars; a custom which probably originated from celebrating on the tombs of martyrs. Under the high altar of Bayeux Cathedral, previous to the great revolution, were five shrines of silver gilt ; and the frontal of the altar, which was also of silver parcel gilt, was made to open on certain great festivals, like two doors, to show the reliquaries.

‡ The curtains hung in front of shrines, under the ancient altars, are undoubtedly the origin of antependiums or frontals, for we find examples of such curtains in the earliest records of altars, which were made to run on a rod fixed immediately under the slab.

Behind the altar is a succession of lancet stone arches, the panels of which are richly diapered and ornamented with Christian emblems : the painted window over them, as well as the catherine-wheel window at the top, will be filled with mosaic stained glass, with subjects occasionally introduced in small medallion and quarterfoils. The sedilia and sacrarium are of stone, and taken out of the thickness of the wall. The eastern wall of the chancel is four feet in thickness, and the deep splays of the window will be enriched with painted scrolls, in the early style.

A second example is the chancel of St. Mary's, Uttoxeter, (see Pl. XV,) a small church recently completed. Here the altar is of the ancient triptic form,* with doors to be closed during the latter part of Lent; in the centre is a picture of our blessed Lady, copied from one of the true Christian school; on either side are two damask curtains, hung on rods, between which and the altar stand two large candlesticks to hold tapers, lit from the Sanctus to the Communion. The front of the altar is of stone, gilt and painted, with the Crucifixion in the centre, and the emblems of evangelists in the angles. The rood is here supported by an arch beam, with angels bearing tapers. Before the altar hang three lamps, one of which is kept constantly burning, and the other two lit during the celebration of mass. The sedilia are three stone recesses, divided by shafts, and diapered at the back ; opposite to these is an arched recess, for the sepulchre in holy week. The three lancet windows over the altar are filled with stained glass, of an early character, and at the western end is a rose window, very richly glazed.

---

* These triptics were usually placed over altars in the Continental churches ; as at Cologne Cathedral, and several of the German churches, particularly those of St. Lawrence and St. Sebald's ; at Nuremberg they will remain in the most perfect state. The old form remained in use long after the cessation of pointed architecture in these countries, and even down to the time of Rubens. There is a most splendid enamelled triptic of the twelfth century in the Museum of St. Mary's College, Oscott, and the form was commonly employed for all religious pictures, and not unfrequently in wood and ivory carvings. In carved triptics for altars, the sculptured figures are placed immediately over the altar, and the doors are decorated with painting only ; in these latter, the pious donors were frequently painted kneeling at prayer, with their patron saints standing behind them. Although these triptics were not very generally placed over altars in England, still we have instances of their having been used at Melford Church, Suffolk. " At the back of the high altar was set up the story of Christ's Passion, fair gilt and beautifully set forth to cover and keep clean all which *were very fair painted boards, made to shut to, which were opened upon high and solemn feast days.* In Durham Cathedral there was also, standing against the wall, a most curious fine table, with *two leaves to open and shut,* comprehending the Passion of our Lord Jesus Christ, richly cut and fine lively colours, which table was always locked up but on principal days."—*Rites of Durham.*

The third example is the church of St. Giles, Cheadle, (see Pl. XVI.) The whole of the ceiling will be richly painted with azure panels and gilt stars; the string course supporting the ribs is charged with shields and inscriptions. In the stone niches on each side of the window are images of our blessed Lady and St. Giles. Over the altar is a stone screen of tabernacle work, with images of apostles, and our blessed Lord in the centre; on the altar are a pair of candlesticks and an altar cross, with rich hangings, and frontals of various colours. The sacrarium is here formed by a fourth compartment added to the sedilia, which are surmounted by gables and pinnacles, richly foliated. On the north side is an arched tomb for the sepulchre; and the floor will be paved with encrusted tiles, charged with armorial bearings.

OF THE SEDILIA.

On the epistle side of the altar, either on the ascent of the steps leading up to the altar, or on the level pavement, three arched recesses are invariably built, for the officiating priest, deacon, and sub-deacon to sit in during the chanting of the Gloria and Credo.* These sometimes consist of three simple arches, supported either by corbels or shafts; and occasionally we find them richly decorated with canopies and groining. In parochial churches they are generally built of stone, but in the large cathedrals and abbeys they were sometimes of wood. The four arches on the epistle side of the sanctuary of Westminster Abbey, commonly called King Sebert's Tomb, are in fact the sedilia of that church. It is not at all unusual to find a fourth stall, for the assistant priest, in great churches. Among the most beautiful examples of sedilia, remaining in England, we may mention those at Exeter Cathedral, Southwell Minster, Ripon Cathedral, Tewkesbury Abbey, Adderbury and Dorchester Church, Oxfordshire; Bishopston, Wilts; St. Mary's, Oxford; and Stockport Church, near Manchester. These arched recesses have been frequently termed confessionals, by persons unacquainted with ecclesiastical antiquities, but we need hardly observe, without the slightest foundation. The misrepresentations made on this subject, by persons who shew cathedral and other churches, is most extraordinary. Any perforation in a wall, whether it be to admit light or air, or to command a view of the high altar from some chapel, is invariably called a confessional; even the chantry chapel of the Beauchamp family, at Warwick, is so designated.

---

* The priest anciently sat during the Epistle in solemn masses.

It is established even beyond a doubt, that there were no confessionals in our ancient churches answering in form to those we see generally used on the Continent: confessions were heard in the church by priests, seated in chairs, whilst the penitent knelt beside them; this may be seen figured in many ancient illuminations. Even on the Continent no confessional can be found older than the last century, and this is alone sufficient to prove the extreme absurdity of the stories circulated by vergers and others, respecting confessionals in the ancient churches.

OF THE SACRARIUM.

Between the sedilia and the eastern wall of the chancel, a small niche was built, in the bottom of which a basin was hollowed out of the stone, with a pipe leading into the ground; over this was a small projecting stone shelf for the altar cruets. The most ancient sacrariums had two basins, as may be seen by those at Salisbury and Lincoln Cathedrals; one for the ablutions of the hands at the *Lavabo*, and the other for the ablutions of the chalice, which were not received by the priest, as at present, but poured down the sacrarium.

The old rubric respecting the Lavabo is as follows: " Eat ad Piscinam dicens Lavabo: reversus dicit In spiritu humilitatis, &c." This is found in many ancient Missals. When the rubric for receiving the ablutions of the chalice became generally observed, the second basin was disused, and the late sacrariums have one basin only.

OF THE ARCH ON THE GOSPEL SIDE OF THE CHANCEL.

On the gospel side of the chancel, and nearly opposite the sedilia, we generally find an arch forming a recess and canopy to an altar tomb: this was used as a sepulchre for the reservation of the blessed sacrament, from Maunday Thursday till Easter Sunday morning, which was anciently practised in the Sarum rite.* There is frequent allusion to this in the wills of pious persons, who desired to have their tombs so built that

---

* This ceremony is quite distinct from the reservation of the blessed sacrament from Maundy Thursday for the mass of Good Friday, on which day the Church does not allow of any consecration. The blessed sacrament, so reserved, is watched all night, and hence the name of sepulchre has been most improperly given to the chapel in which it is solemnly kept; but there is not the slightest correspondence as to time in the present watching, which takes place on Maundy Thursday night, when our Lord did not suffer till Friday. The watching, according to the Sarum rite, commenced on Good Friday, and continued till Easter-day, early in the morning, when the blessed sacrament was brought forth from the sepulchre with solemn procession. This ceremony was also practised in France and some of the Northern Countries, but there is no trace of it in the Roman rite.

they might serve for the sepulchre; that when men came to pay their devotions to our Lord's body, at that holy time, they might be moved to pray for the repose of their souls. At Long Melford Church, Suffolk, the tomb of one of the Clopton family served for this purpose. Some of the finest examples of stone sepulchres are at Eckington Church, Lincolnshire, and Hawton Church, Nottinghamshire; these are richly decorated in the style of Edward III, with representations of the Roman soldiers asleep, and other appropriate imagery.

OF THE REVESTRY OR SACRISTRY.

It is a remarkable fact, that while sacristies in most cathedral churches were placed on the south side, in parish churches they were generally built on a contrary one. We are quite at a loss to assign any reason for this; as a southern aspect would be most suitable to prevent damp or injury to the vestments. Although most of the ancient fittings of church vestries have been destroyed, we may occasionally find a few old almeries remaining,* but not one vestige of the rich furniture and sacred vessels with which they were filled.†

OF THE ALTAR.

During the first seven centuries of the Church, altars were made indifferently of wood, stone, and metal.‡

Doubtless, during the early persecutions of the Christians,

---

* At Adderbury Church, Oxon ; Long Melford, Suffolk ; Wells Cathedral ; York Minster ; in a side Chapel at Carlisle Cathedral·

† In *Lyndwood's Provinciale* we find the following inventory of ornaments required in every parish church:—"Legendam, Antiphonarium, Graduale, Psalterium, Troperium Ordinale, Missale, Manuale, Calicem, Vestimentum Principale cum casula, Dalmatica, Tunica, et cum capa in Choro, cum omnibus suis appendiciis; Frontale ad Magnum altare cum tribus Tuellis, tria supepellicia, unum Rochetum, Crucem Processionalem, Crucem pro Mortuis, Thuribulum, Lucernam, Tintinabulum ad deferendum coram corpore Christi in visitatione infirmorum, Pyxidem pro corpore Christi, honestum Velum Quadragesimale, Campanis cum chordis, Feretrum pro defunctis, Vas pro Aqua Benedicta, Osculatorium Candelabrum pro cereo paschali, Fontem cum serura, Imagines in ecclesia, Imaginem principalem in cancello."

To these may be added a lettern, or brass eagle, to stand in the chancel or choir, for the antiphonarium and graduals. A most beautiful brass lettern of this description was lying, only two years since, in a corner of the tower of St. Martin's Church, Salisbury, utterly neglected, and most probably considered a piece of old Popish lumber.

‡ The Emperor Constantine made seven altars of silver in the Church called after his name, and that of St. John Lateran, which weighed 260lbs. Sixtus III. gave an altar of pure silver, which weighed 300lbs., to the Church of St. Mary Major. St. Athanasius speaks of an altar of wood which the Arians burnt. St. Sylvester I. is said to have forbidden all wooden altars, except that in St. John Lateran's (yet existing), because St. Peter had used it.

altars were generally of wood, as being more portable, and better adapted to the necessities of the time.

Since the seventh century, the use of stone altars in the Church has not only been universal, but obligatory, insomuch that no priest would be allowed to celebrate without, at least, a portable altar stone.

The use of portable altar stones is very ancient; Jonas, monk of St. Wandrille, is the first writer by whom they are mentioned, in the Life of St. Wulfran, where it is recorded that this holy man carried a consecrated stone with him to celebrate on it in his travels, and afterwards gave it to the Abbey of St. Wandrille. " Altare consecratum in quatuor angulorum locis et in medio; reliquias continens sanctorum in modum clypie etc." Portable altars are also mentioned by the venerable Bede, when speaking of the two Ewalds: "Cotidie Sacrificium Deo victimæ salutaris offerebant, habentes secum vascula ad *tabulam altaris* vice dedicatam."

The use of portable altars was however confined to journeys and cases of *great necessity*; they were *neither meant nor suffered to replace or supersede the stone altars which are required by the Church, and which should be erected in every permanent religious edifice.*

The most ancient altars were open underneath, and supported by pillars : every altar should be sufficiently detached from the wall to admit of passing behind it. The ceremonies of the consecration of an altar, in the Roman pontifical, require the bishop to pass round the altar various times. " *Pontifex circuit septies tabulam altaris aspergens eam et stipitem de aqua ultimo per eum benedicta, &c.*" That the most ancient altars were all detached from the wall is evident by the language of the early ecclesiastical writers.

Excepting during the celebration of the holy sacrifice, neither cross nor candlesticks were formerly left on the altar, but were removed immediately after mass. The book of the holy gospels was alone kept on the altar.*

---

* It does not appear that any cross was placed *on* the altar before the tenth century. The crosses were fixed *over* the altars, and on the ciboriums or canopies, by which they were surmounted : neither was the image of our Lord crucified attached to these crosses. The crucifix was, however, set up on the rood as early as the eighth century; and it was probably on account of the blessed sacrament lying on the altar that the ancient Churchmen would not suffer an image in the presence of the reality ; even the present rubric speaks only of a cross on the altar, *crux in medio.* No lights were placed on the altar before the tenth century, and even down to the French revolution, many of the most ancient and illustrious Churches of that country did not admit of any

Before the twelfth century flowers were not suffered on altars, although the custom of hanging garlands and branches, on great feasts, to decorate the church, is of the highest antiquity: even the whole pavement was not unfrequently sprinkled with flowers and aromatic herbs.

It does not appear that even the relics of saints were allowed *on* the ancient altars, especially in presence of the blessed sacrament. Shrines, with relics, were placed under the altars, and on a beam over the altar.*

The blessed srcrament was never reserved at the high altar of a church excepting in a golden dove, or pyx, suspended over the altar.† Mass was never celebrated formerly in presence of the blessed sacrament, even when enclosed in a tower or tabernacle.

lights *on the high* altars, but placed round them. Wax tapers were lit in large candlesticks on each side of the altar, hung on prickets in basins before it, and in coronas, or large circles of lights, in the choir, on the *jubé* or rood loft, before images, and near shrines, but not on the altars.

* This was the case at Canterbury cathedral.

+ The custom of reserving the blessed sacrament in gold and silver doves is very ancient. Perpetuus VI., archbishop of Tours, left a silver dove to a priest, Amalarius, for this purpose, "Peristerium et columbam argenteam ad repositorium." In the customs of the monastery of Cluny, a dove of gold is mentioned suspended over the altar in which the blessed Eucharist was reserved. This custom was retained till the revolution at the Church of St. Julien d'Angers, St. Maur des Fosses, near Paris, at St. Paul, Sens, at St. Lierche, near Chartres.

" The blessed sacrament was suspended in a pyx, over the high altar at Durham abbey. Within the quire, over the high altar, hung a rich and most sumptuous canopy for the blessed sacrament to hang within it, which had two irons fastened in the French trieme very finely gilt; which held the canopy over the midst of the said high altar that the pyx hung in, that it could neither move nor stir; whereon stood a pelican all of silver, upon the height of the said canopy, very finely gilt, giving her blood to her young ones, in token that Christ gave his blood for the sins of the world; and it was goodly to behold for the blessed sacrament to hang in. And the pyx wherein the blessed sacrament hung was of most pure gold, curiously wrought of goldsmith's work; and the white cloth that hung over the pyx was of very fine lawn, all embroidered and wrought about with gold and red silk, and four great round knobs of gold curiously wrought, with great tassels of gold and red silk hung at them; and the crook that hung within the cloth that the pyx hung upon was of gold, and the cord which drew it up and down was made of fine strong silk."—*Rites of Durham.*

" French Churches in which the blessed sacrament was suspended in a pyx, before the revolution: St. Maurile d'Angers, Cathedrale de Tours, St. Martin de Tours, St. Siran en Brenne, St. Etienne de Dijon, St. Sieur de Dijon, St. Etienne de Sens, Cathedrale de St. Julien, Mons, Nôtre Dame de Chartres, Nôtre Dame de Paris, St. Ouen de Rouen."—*De Moleon, Voyage Liturgique.*

Matthew Paris speaks of the blessed sacrament being suspended over the high altar of the cathedral Church of Lincoln.—Ad an. 1140. *In Stephano.*

It was doubtless in allusion to these doves that St. John Chrysostom says, the sacred body of our Lord in the Churches is not enveloped in linen, as in the cradle, but in the form of the *Holy Spirit.*

The present tabernacles are by no means ancient, nor did they exist in the old English churches.

The blessed sacrament was either reserved as above-mentioned, in a dove, or a small metal tabernacle in the form of a tower. These towers* are frequently mentioned by old ecclesiastical writers.

St. Renis, archbishop of Rheims, ordered by his will that his successor should make a tabernacle in the form of a tower, weighing ten marks of gold.

Fortunat, bishop of Poitiers, eulogised St. Felix, archbishop of Bruges, for causing a precious tower of gold to be made for the sacred body of our Lord.

Frodoard, priest of Rheims, relates that Landon, archbishop of that see, placed a tower of gold on an altar of the cathedral, for the reservation of the blessed Eucharist.

The fronts of altars were ornamented by antependiums of rich stuffs, of various colours, richly embroidered on panels of silver, parcel gilt and enamelled, and even occasionally set with precious stones. In the inventory of the ornaments of Lincoln Minster, given in Dugdale's *Monasticon*, we find above thirty frontals of velvet and silk, some exceedingly costly. "Imprimis, a costly cloth of gold for the high altar, for principal feasts, having in the midst images of the Holy Trinity, of our Lady, four evangelists, four angels about the Trinity, with patriarchs, prophets, apostles, virgins, with many other images; having a frontlet of cloth of gold, with Scriptures, and a linen cloth infixed to the same, *ex dono Ducis Lancastriæ*."

There were frontals of precious metals at Rheims Cathedral,

---

* The new Churches of St Ann's, Keighley; St. Mary's, Uttoxeter; St Wilfred's, Manchester; St. Alban's, Macclesfield; St. Chad's, Birmingham; St. Mary's, Dudley, are all furnished with these towers, instead of modern tabernacles. There is but little doubt that in many of our small parish Churches the blessed Eucharist was reserved in a strong almery, on the gospel side of the chancel. In Germany and Belgium several magnificent tabernacles of stone, carried up to a prodigious height, and equisitely wrought, remain on the gospel side of the choir. Those at St. Lawrence's Church, Nuremberg, and the Cathedral at Ulm, executed by Adam Kraft, are the most beautiful. A tabernacle of this description is still used for its original sacred purpose in the Cathedral of Louvain; but how long this remnant of ancient practice may remain is most uncertain, for the destroying spirit of novelty has already run riot in this once glorious church. The beautiful triptic, over the high altar, has been pulled down and sold, and a wretched marble mass of columns and cornices erected in its stead; the sedilia *demolished;* the unrivalled brass lectorium sold out of the choir; the altars of the choir screen taken away, and the choir thrown open to the nave; and the glorious tabernacle itself menaced with destruction, on account, forsooth, of its being placed on one side of the Church.

the Abbey of St. Ouen, Rouen; St. Germain des Prés, Paris, St. Mark's, Venice; Bayeux Cathedral, and many other churches.

Round the most ancient altars curtains were hung, and closely drawn from the consecration till the communion; this usage was common to both the eastern and western Churches. St. John Chrysostom bears ample testimony to the former, when he says, "that the sacred host is on the altar, and the victim immolated, and these words are pronounced (*Sancta Sanctis*). When the *curtain and veils* are drawn, it seems as if the heavens themselves were opened and the angels descended." (*Hom.* iii. *in Epist. ad Ephes.*) As for the western Church, we read in the lives of many popes,* that they caused curtains of precious stuffs to be hung round the altars of various churches in Rome.

It does not appear that curtains were ever hung *entirely round* the altars in *England,* but *invariably at the sides,* and sometimes at the back. These were called dossels, and are mentioned in the inventory of St. Osmund's Church, at Old Sarum. A curtain or veil was also hung over the imagery, at back of the altars, during Lent. The side curtains remained in use in England till the destruction of the altars, under Edward VI; and in France, in many of the large churches, till the great revolution.

We have already mentioned that previous to the tenth century candles were not placed upon the altar, and from that period down to the sixteenth century the number was generally restricted to two.† The usual number of six is a comparatively modern usage, even at Rome, and the rubric of the Roman missal only requires two lights during the celebration of the Holy Eucharist: " Super altare collocetur crux in medio et candelabra saltem duo cum candelis accensis hinc et inde in utroque ejus latere."

Every altar should be built of stone: the top slab of one piece with five crosses cut on it—one at each angle and in the

---

* Sergius I, Gregory III, Adrian I, Leo III, Pascal I, Gregory IV, Sergius II, Leo IV, and Nicholas I. "In circuitu altaris tetravela octo; per altaris circuitum vela de rhodino quatuor quæ sacrum altare circumdant. Contulit in basilica apostolorum cortinam lineam unam, velotyra, serica tria, in circuitu altaris."

† Although only two candlesticks were placed on the altar, these were occasionally made to hold several candles, which were doubtless lit on great festivals. In the inventory of the ornaments of Lincoln: " Item, two condlesticks of silver parcel gilt, standing on great feet, with *six towers* gilded, having one great knob in the midst, and in the height six towers about the bowls, with one pike of silver *on either of them.*"

centre; the whole of this stone should be consecrated by the bishop, instead of a portable altar being inserted in it, which should only be tolerated in a case of the greatest necessity. The front of the altar, if solid, should be furnished with, at least, an antependium with appropriate ornaments, and a purple frontal for Lent; but, if means would permit, a complete set of frontals of the five colours should be provided. Three linen cloths are required for covering the altar stone : the first is the cere cloth, waxed all over, and made to fit over the stone exactly; this is never removed. The second of fine linen, plain, the length and width of the stone, to lie over the cere cloth. The third should be sufficiently long to hang down at each end of the altar to the pavement; this should be marked with five crosses, and may be ornamented at the ends with needle-work.

A pair of curtains should be hung on each side of the altar, nearly of the same projection from the wall; these should be varied in colour to that of the festival; but, as means will not generally permit of so doing, crimson for ordinary use, with purple for Lent, will be sufficient.

These curtains should be hung sufficiently high to protect the candles from wind, and reach nearly to the ground.

Nothing but the candlesticks, cross, and a small tower for the reservation of the blessed sacrament, should be placed on the altar.

The screen, or dossell, is the proper position for the images of the saints; their relics may repose beneath the sacrificial stone, the walls may be hung with flowers and wreaths, but the altar should be free and unincumbered for the holy sacrifice. All the ancient discipline that we have quoted tended to this point.

The form and ornaments of altars are not matters of mere whim and caprice, but of antiquity and authority; their purpose is far too sacred to admit of their being made the vehicles of paltry display and meretricious ornament.* Yet every reflecting mind must be both struck and pained with the incongruous decorations of most of the modern altars; the chief

---

* It should always be remembered that the ceremonies of the Church are *realities*, not *representations;* that they are instituted not to *dazzle the eye* but *to honour God.* Altars are not meant to be merely seen by man, but should be erected to meet the all-searching eye of God. The holy of holies, under the old law, in which no man except the high-priest entered, was overlaid with gold;— and should our sanctuary for the reality be less splendid than that of the figure? Surely not. Hence gilding and ornament should not be always *turned towards the people,* nor a showy antependium conceal dirt and neglect.

aim of those who arrange them appears to be merely a great show. All mystical reasons, all ancient discipline,* all dignity and solemnity are utterly lost sight of; everything is over-done. Candlesticks are piled on candlesticks as if arranged for sale; whole rows of flower pots mingled with reliquaries, images, and not unfrequently profane ornaments; festoons of upholsterers' drapery : even distorting and distracting looking-glasses are introduced in this medley display ; the effect of which upon persons who are conversant with ancient discipline and practice it is not easy to describe.

Of all decoration, that of ecclesiastical buildings is the most difficult ; to unite *richness* with *severity,* to produce *splendour* without *gaudiness,* and to erect a temple somewhat worthy of the holy sacrifice, is a wonderful effort for the human mind: but when decoration is attempted in honour of the victim there offered—the blessed Sacrament itself—art droops unequal, and genius fails. Who is there that can set forth the glory of God, or add lustre to His majesty? The attempt is almost profane. Hence the ancient churchmen veiled the sacred host in mystery, and, like Moses before the burning bush, bowed themselves to the ground. If the faithful are required to adore in silence, during the elevation of the host, as being too solemn a moment for even the psalmody of praise, " Sileat omnis caro a facie Domini quia consurrexit de habitaculo Sancto suo," what forms can be embodied to honour so great a mystery ?

The arrangements sometimes made for this purpose are more calculated to throw ridicule on the solemnity than to raise feelings of inward reverence, and however well meant are not the less objectionable. Lights alone can be considered appro-

---

* The greatest innovation of later times is placing altars *all over a church;* formerly they were strictly confined to the eastern ends, and *all protected by screens* in regular chapels. *The mass is not less holy, adorable, and deserving of respect because it is celebrated at an altar which is not the principal one of the church :* the same reasons which require *that* to be screened off from the people, *apply equally to the others.* Now we not only find many altars without screens in modern churches, but *erected against pillars of the nave,* where a great portion of the people must turn their backs on the sacrifice there offered. The nave is erected *for the faithful,* and not as a place wherein to *celebrate the holy mysteries;* the very fact of altars having been erected in such a position, shews how completely the mystical reasons which regulated the architecture and arrangement of ancient catholic Churches, have been lost sight of; and hence arises the gross irreverence to be witnessed on the Continent during the celebration of masses at these altars, and is another proof of the intimate connexion between the externals of religion and internal effect on the mind.

priate emblems near the blessed Eucharist, for they have ever been used by the Church as marks of honour, and figures of the brightness and glory of God : and even these require much judgment in their distribution, inclining more on the side of humble simplicity than of pretension towards an unattainable end ; and (like the painter, who, unable to represent the intense grief of the human mind, covered the visage of his figure), confess our inability to *embody* our veneration for the adorable mystery, and substitute for ornament a veil.

It is proper to remark, that all the altars in the churches of which we have given engravings have been erected and decorated with scrupulous regard to the ancient tradition.

We fear we cannot assert, from the examples which we have brought forward, that the English Catholics, as *a body*, are reviving Catholic architecture, for such is unhappily far from the case at present ; but we have brought forward sufficient examples to shew that it is *quite possible for them, in the nineteenth century, to revive the ecclesiastical glories of the days of faith*, and it is merely owing to their energies not being sufficiently directed to this important object, that much greater restorations are not achieved. If the piety, faith, and zeal of bygone times are revived, then equal results will soon be attained. There is, at the present time, a great and increasing feeling of admiration for old Catholic art ; and among those who have greatly contributed to revive this love of Catholic antiquity, are certain learned members of the Establishment, resident at Oxford ; whose endeavours, in this cause, entitle them to the respect and gratitude of all who are anxious to behold a restoration of our ancient solemn churches. Some papers which have appeared in the *British Critic* on this subject, have been written by one who truly feels the principles which actuated the ancient builders in their designs. So much respect indeed do we entertain for the writer in question, that we are pained in being compelled to act as his opponent, although it be only for a time : still the *exclusive* tone he has assumed is so fallacious, that it becomes a duty to point out the inconsistency of it. We repeat we are truly grateful for all the Oxford men have done, and are doing, towards the revival of Catholic art and antiquity : still, hampered as they are by parliamentary restrictions, and their Protestant associates, they can accomplish but little in these respects, compared with what a handful of English Catholics have done who work on the ancient foundation.

We both descend from ancestors who professed one faith

as members of the old Catholic Church of England. The Establishment are the many who, converted by political intriguers, avaricious and ambitious men, abandoned the faith of their fathers, and received parliamentary enactments for the decrees of the Church. The English Catholics are the few who remained witnesses of the truth, under the severest trials of persecution.

The Establishment, although she started strong and mighty, is now miserably fallen; she has existed long enough to suffer the most bitter degradations at the hands of her own nominal children: and having lost the hearts and control of the people—distracted by dissensions—betrayed by false brethren —the learned and pious of her communion look back with longing regret on the happy state of England's Church, ere political intriguers had forced it into schism, and separated it from the communion of the Christian world. Under these circumstances we should have hoped, and expected, that the feeling of deep humility (so beautifully expressed in an article on the Church service in the *British Critic*) would have influenced the tone of the writer on church architecture; but this, we are sorry to perceive, is far from the case. We cannot understand how a church in the old English style, erected by the descendants of those who retained the practice of the old rites, can be a *painful* object* to one *professing Catholic principles;* nor why he should be *edified* (even supposing such were the case) that the new Catholic church and dissenting meeting-house were built in the same manner: unless he were influenced by party feelings, such a falling off should cause his sincere grief. Far be it from us to exult at the abortions raised by the Establishment for her worship; it is on the contrary a subject of deep lamentation, that any persons whose ancestors were members of the Catholic Church should have so wofully deserted from the spirit of antiquity. And on the other hand, when we behold even the intention of restoring Catholic architecture and practices, we are both edified and thankful that such feelings should exist.

We are willing to admit that the modern externals of Catholicism in this country are but little calculated to impress a casual observer with feelings of religious veneration, but as the English Catholics have been driven from every ancient church, and cut off from old associations, their present condition, in these respects, is less astonishing than that of the

---

* " This is indeed a *painfully* beautiful structure."

members of the Establishment, who, with the glories of the old edifices continually before them, have not only departed from every ancient practice, but have defaced and destroyed, in a great measure, the most beautiful portions of these venerable edifices.

It is true that the feelings of many of her children are Catholic, but the Establishment is decidedly Protestant. How would the parochial churches, in their present state, bear the test of an old English episcopal visitation? A solitary surplice and tattered prayer book would but ill answer to the long catalogue of sacred vessels and ornaments extracted from *Lyndwood's Provinciale.* The unoccupied sedilia; the broken sacrarium; the defaced screen, denuded of its emblem of redemption; the dismounted altar stone, trampled under foot; the damp and mouldering chancel; the broken window and uptorn brass, would but ill exhibit that love of Anglican rites, which the writer would fain usurp as the exclusive feeling of the Establishment: and yet this is the state of almost every church in the country, which is not fortunate enough to have an Oxford man for its incumbent: and then, however good may be his intentions, he is so restricted and controlled, that he can do little more than remove some coats of whitewash, and open a blocked-up arch or window. It is a fact, and we say it in sorrow—not exultation, that there is not a single church, in the possession of the Establishment, where *any* of the old Anglican rites are preserved. There is a great deal written respecting them, it is true, but where are the actual results? Do the clergy celebrate in the ancient vestments? Do they burn lights on the altars and near the tombs of the martyrs? Do they venerate the remains of the saints? Do they place hallowed water in the porches of the churches? Are the roods rested over the screens? Are the sedilia occupied by the clergy? For these are all practices of remote antiquity. It is a striking fact, that *Anglican* rites were in use in the Church of England only so *long as she retained her canonical obedience to the holy see, and ceased with her schism.*

A paper has recently appeared, on the Anglo-Catholic use of two lights at the altar, the object of which is excellent; but it is well known that this disuse of the Anglo-Catholic practice is *exactly coeval* with the *formation of the present Establishment,* as they were utterly disused after the short-lived reign of the first book of common prayer. We had in England, from Saxon times downwards, our own missals, rituals, benedictionals, offices, litanies, which included among the most ancient Catholic rites, *some exclusively English*, with vast privileges; and yet all these Anglican rites were abolished to introduce *Lutheran and Genevan discipline, when England's Church was brought under the yoke of foreign sectaries*, by the so-called reformers of the sixteenth century. And if these Anglican rites have in some respects been suspended amongst us, who are the remnant of the whole faith, is it not owing to our having been so deserted and persecuted by our Protestant countrymen that we have been too depressed and divided to keep up the externals and practice of a Church? But, however we may fall short in these respects when compared with the glories of ancient days, we are still wonderfully in advance of the members of the Establishment, who, still writhing under the evil influence of a Peter Martyr and John a Lasco, are unable to revive a single practice of Anglo-catholic antiquity. It ill becomes them to speak in a taunting manner of our deficiencies in these respects, and to make extravagant deductions from accidental contingencies; we allude particularly to the observations made on the position of the church at Derby.*

---

* There is not the slightest foundation for the *significant relation*, asserted by the reviewer, between the church at Derby and the Roman basilicas; there is not, in fact, the smallest similarity between the two. In the basilica, the altar and the celebrant *face the east and the people*, of which we are not aware of any other instance. At Derby, the building was unfortunately forced into a south and north position. The church at Moorfields was erected by a Protestant, who was totally ignorant of any canonical regulation, and was far more influenced by the city commissioners, in not *spoiling the uniformity of the crescent*, than any notions of introducing Roman discipline into London. As for Mr. Fletcher's meeting-house, the mention of which is rather insultingly introduced, the reviewer must be aware that it has no *bearing at all*, there being neither end nor side, but one great galleried preaching house, with benches all round; a vile conventicle, which, we should have thought, any one *professing Catholic feelings* would not have named in conjunction with a church, built on the same site and position, and over the same sacred tombs, as one of the oldest edifices devoted to Christian worship.

There is one observation of the reviewer in which we most heartily concur—the absence of altars at the extremities of the aisles is a *great* defect, although not an *irremediable* one; and we shall hope, before long, to see these, as well as a regular chancel screen, and other arrangements which are absolutely required to be completed, in order to perfect the interior of this edifice.

We cannot conclude these observations without expressing our perfect concurrence in the views of the writer, respecting the propriety and necessity of adhering to the ancient traditional position of churches, from west to east; and we hold, that nothing short of absolute necessity could palliate, even in these times, any departure from this practice. But few persons are acquainted with the difficulties to be encountered in procuring land for the erection of Catholic churches. No sooner does the intention of commencing such a structure become known, than every engine of prejudice and interest is brought to bear in opposition, and sites are sometimes purchased, through necessity, which will not possibly admit of canonical arrangements in the position of the edifice.

D

Had the writer examined the dimensions of the site, he must at once have perceived that the uncanonical position of the building was occasioned, not through disrespect for the ancient tradition of Christendom—which we revere most highly ; not from any idea of introducing Roman peculiarities in England, but from unavoidable necessity, occasioned by want of space, from west to east.   Had the church been properly placed, even supposing the whole width of the land occupied, not only would the light of both eastern and western windows have been at the mercy of the adjacent proprietors, but the edifice itself would have been much too short for its required purposes. Every expedient, by placing the tower on the side, &c., was tried, but was reluctantly and of necessity abandoned.

The annexed plan will shew these difficulties ; and it will also be seen that the church was brought forward to its present

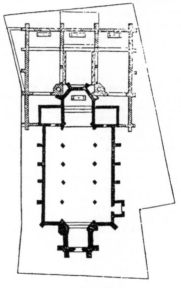

DERBY.*

position to admit of enlarging the chancel, and adding chapels towards the altar end.

---

* As the exterior and interior of this church have been already etched in two plates, published by Dolman, and also illustrated in the "British Critic," it has not been considered necessary to introduce them in this article.

It was certainly a lamentable necessity which compelled the architect to turn the church at Derby towards the north; but yet this is a light defect, when compared with the pewing of St. Alkmund's, where, in a canonically-built church, the congregation not only face the north, but sit in hollow squares and galleries, and *face each other*. The writer could not have selected a more unfortunate example for illustrating the love of Catholic antiquity in the Establishment, than this ancient but desecrated edifice : it is an old Catholic shell, cut up, galleried, defaced, and transformed by every description of Protestant monstrosity, from the Genevan reading-desk, down to the *glazed* and cushioned pew of the last century. But mistaken indeed are the ideas of the reviewer, in imagining that the new church of St. Mary's was erected as if in *hostile opposition* to the venerable fabric of St. Alkmund's; for, desecrated and desolated as it stands, the pious Catholic can gaze with feelings of deep veneration on an edifice from whose tower the bells have oft called the people to early sacrifice, and beneath whose ancient pavement repose the remains of many a faithful soul departed. How little can the writer estimate the feelings of a true English Catholic, if he thinks every stone of the ancient churches is not inestimably dear to him; for, independent of the art and science of their construction, their antiquity alone will awaken associations more holy and consoling, than the most splendid . revivals of Catholic art in the present day can produce. It is a strange inconsistency in such men as the reviewer, to misrepresent and disparage the intentions and works of the only body who are capable of carrying out the very ideas he so beautifully expresses. We are quite willing to throw overboard such of the modern Catholic erections as are built without reference to canonical arrangement or the traditions of the Church, to be dealt with as unmercifully as the conventicles which they much resemble. But we protest against charging the whole body with the ignorance of some of its members; and we equally object to the writer claiming Catholic feelings for the Establishment, as a *body*, because such good sentiments have revived among a few of its members. By how small a proportion would the sentiments of the reviewer be *even understood*, and by a how much smaller proportion *appreciated as they deserve*. The very truth contained in his article refutes the position he would attempt to claim. Everything Catholic in England is at so low an ebb at present, that it is folly to boast. All we contend for is, that Catholicism in this country possesses sufficient internal strength to revive its ancient glory; while the Establishment, however willing some of its members may be to produce such a result, cannot, under its present system, achieve it. And why is this? It is not from any want of piety, zeal, learning, disinterestedness, or holiness of life,—for all these requisites are possessed in a high degree by many among them; it is simply for want of a really Catholic foundation. If reunited in communion with the rest of the Christian world, and absolved from the censures which their forefathers incurred, how rapidly would they achieve the greatest works! The spirit of the ancient churchmen breathes in their writings, and in their deeds,—but, like the green shoots from a prostrate trunk, wanting a source, fail in producing fruit; and the men who, in better days, would have raised a Lincoln or founded a Winchester, are scarcely able to preserve common decency of worship, or arrest increasing decay, in the churches which they serve.

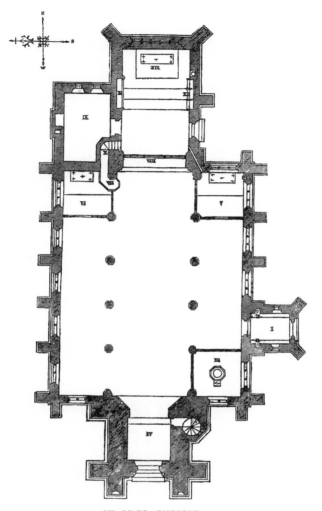

Pl. 1.

ST. GILES, CHEADLE.

I. Porch	VIII. Screen and Rood
II. Holy water stoups	IX. Sacristy
III. Font and Baptistery	X. Staircase to Rood
IV. Tower	XI. Sepulchre
V. St. Mary's Chapel	XII. Sedilia
VI. St. John's Chapel	XIII. High altar
VII. Pulpit	

Pl. II.

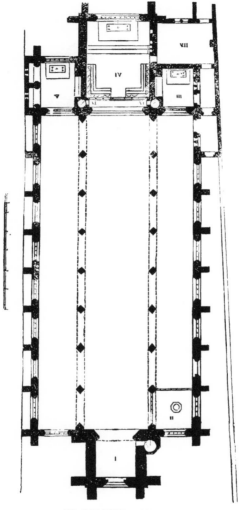

ST. GEORGE'S, LONDON.

i. Tower
ii. Baptistery and Font
iii. St. Mary's Chapel
iv. Chancel
v. Chapel of the holy Trinity
vi. Staircases to Rood
vii. Sacristy

Pl. III.

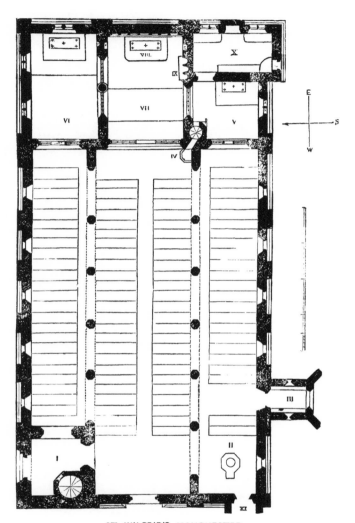

ST. WILFRID'S, MANCHESTER.

I. Tower	VI. St. Mary's Chapel
II. Font	VII. Chancel
III. Porch	VIII. High altar
IV. Pulpit	IX. Sedilia
V. St. Thomas's Chapel	X. Sacristy

Pl. IV.

ST. GILES', CHEADLE.

Pl. V.

ST. GEORGE'S, LONDON.

Pl. VI.

ST. OSWALD'S, LIVERPOOL.

Pl. VII.

ST. WILFRID'S, MANCHESTER.

ST. MARY'S, DUDLEY.

Pl. VIII.

STOCKTON-ON-TEES.

Pl. IX.

ST. ANNE'S, KEIGHLEY.

ST. MARY'S, SOUTHPORT.

Pl. **X**.

ST. MARY'S-ON-THE-SANDS, SOUTHPORT.

Pl. XI.

ST. ALBAN'S, MACCLESFIELD.

Pl. XII.

ST. GEORGE'S FIELDS, LONDON.

Pl. XIII.

ST. GILES', CHEADLE.

Pl. XIV.

CHANCEL OF ST. WILFRID'S, MANCHESTER.

Pl. XV.

ST. MARY'S, UTTOXETER.

Pl. XVI.

CHANCEL OF ST. GILES', CHEADLE.

ON THE PRESENT STATE OF

ECCLESIASTICAL ARCHITECTURE
IN ENGLAND.

———

ARTICLE THE SECOND.

From the DUBLIN REVIEW, No. XXIII.
February 1842.

ECCLESIASTICAL ARCHITECTURE
IN ENGLAND.

ART. III.—1. *A Few Words to Churchwardens, Nos.* 1 *and* 2.
*A Few Words to Churchbuilders. A Few Hints on the
Practical Study of Ecclesiastical Antiquities. The Ecclesi-
ologist, Nos.* 1 *and* 2 ; *being all publications of the Cambridge
Camden Society.*

2. *Two Lectures on the Structure and Decorations of Churches.*
By the Rev. G. A. Poole, M.A.

THE increase of public attention to the subject of ecclesiastical antiquities, is one of the most consoling signs of
the present times; not that the mere study of pointed architecture is any novelty, but the present views on this important
subject are far more satisfactory than those which prevailed
but a short time since.

Most elaborate works on the antiquities and topography of
this country, faithful delineations, and correct historical accounts of its most interesting monuments, are indeed abundant,
and as works of practical utility and useful reference cannot
be too strongly commended. But still these partook but little
of the ancient spirit, nor did they materially conduce in imparting it to others; they treated upon Stonehenge, and Lincoln
minster, a Roman encampment, and a parochial church, in the
same tone; they were written, for the most part, more with
a view of preserving the remembrance of past glories than
reviving their execution, and seemed to treat the productions
of our Catholic forefathers as belonging to a state of things
utterly gone by, and never to return. Frequently, indeed,
the grossest discrepancies are to be found between the text
and the subject treated upon. How often the most glorious
monuments of ancient piety are mentioned only for the purpose of defaming the religion and intentions of their holy

founders! How exceedingly painful in this respect are the otherwise meritorious works of Mr. Britton and many others, of which those portions of the text not devoted to mere architectural descriptions, are one tissue of calumnies against the ancient churchmen of this country, and the faith which they so zealously and worthily maintained.

A far better spirit has at length arisen; and we may truly say, that the Cambridge Camden Society have already done, and are actually doing, immense service in the good cause by the admirable publications they are issuing on this subject, some of which we have selected at the head of this article. They do not treat the ecclesiastical antiquities of this country as mere architectural curiosities; or pointed architecture as a matter of arbitrary taste; neither do they hold learned comparisons on the relative beauties of a Corinthian column and a clustered pillar; but they set forth the construction and decoration of the temples dedicated to God in the true light, as matters of Catholic tradition, and propose the ancient Catholic structures as the only models for imitation. Now we do not hesitate in saying, that they have already achieved more practical good by their unpretending publications, than has been accomplished by the united exertions of the antiquaries of the last half century; for they have brought long-forgotten facts before the parties who ought to be especially reminded of them, but who hitherto have known and cared the least about those matters; and it is well known, while Gough was publishing his great work on monumental antiquities, the sextons were ripping up the brasses for sale; and not unfrequently, while an elaborate plate of some interesting portion of a church was preparing for publication, the clergymen or churchwardens of the place were occupied in demolishing it. Although these works are of course addressed to the members of the Anglican Church, yet they cannot be too strongly recommended to the study and attention of the English Catholics, who, owing to their long exclusion from the sacred buildings raised by their ancestors in faith, have wofully departed from the principles which influenced them in the erection of their religious buildings. Before proceeding to examine the works in detail, we must give one extract to show the high Catholic view in which these writers regard the material structure of the ancient churches.

" We enter the Church militant by Holy Baptism : therefore the font is placed by the entrance of the west end : a church built upon the foundation of the apostles and prophets, just as the earthly building is supported by the massive pillars of the nave : we pass along this, keeping our eyes on the passion of Christ depicted at the eastern end, and trusting to the merits of his sacrifice as represented by the altar, till we arrive at the close of life, imaged by the chancel arch and dome ; this we pass through faith, some typical representation of which is usually to be traced in this arch, as the blessed saints and martyrs have gone before us, whose forms are depicted in the roodscreen ; and thus enter the Church triumphant, represented by the chancel."

What can be more consoling than to find the edifying symbolism of our ancient churches thus beautifully recognized and set forth by those who, but a few years since, were foremost in their destruction ? Our joy would indeed be far greater, if all amongst us were able and willing to join in these ideas, and practically revive them. But to proceed. The first tract is addressed to the churchwardens of rural parishes, and is written in a plain, clear style, so that the instructions may be readily understood by those for whom they are intended. It commences with some excellent admonitions relative to the positive duty of preserving and restoring all that is connected with the service of God ; and then proceeds to point out the many causes of that lamentable decay so generally observable in ancient churches, and with advice as to the means of remedying those defects, and preventing further destruction. We then have some very proper censures on those who venture to remove fonts from their ancient position near the western end, to suit their own convenience and caprice, and the gross inconsistency of administering the sacrament of Baptism in the chancel or holy place. The remarks respecting roofs are so very true, and so important, that we have given the extract in full. A high pitched roof is in itself a great ornament to a building, and adds prodigiously to its grandeur ; it prevailed till the decline of pointed architecture, when it fell like the curve of the arches, and with it half the dignity of our ecclesiastical buildings. Let any one compare the effect of such buildings as Lincoln, Westminster, Amiens, and others which retain their original high-pointed roofs, with the latter buildings, where the roofs are flat in pitch, and consequently invisible from below, and they will soon perceive that the former are twice as majestic as the latter. There cannot be a more striking example of this than the nave of Westminster and Henry the Seventh's chapel, where the parapet and pinnacles detaching on the sky look painfully meagre, while the parapet of the Abbey nave, owing to the high roof rising behind it, produces an excellent effect. Nine-tenths of our finest churches have lost half their beauty owing to the destruction of the high roofs with which they were once sumounted, and which have been replaced by low pitched coverings. We now give the words of the tract on this subject.

" It may not be amiss now to say something about the roof. There are few churches which have not lost much of their beauty from their roofs being of a much lower pitch than they used to be. If you look at the east side of your tower, you may see what is called the *weather moulding* of the old roof remaining ; and from thence you will be able to judge how much lower the roof is than it was once. Now the reason is very plain. In this figure, *ABC*

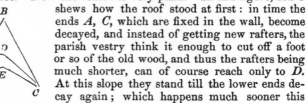 shews how the roof stood at first : in time the ends *A*, *C*, which are fixed in the wall, become decayed, and instead of getting new rafters, the parish vestry think it enough to cut off a foot or so of the old wood, and thus the rafters being much shorter, can of course reach only to *D*. At this slope they stand till the lower ends decay again ; which happens much sooner this time, because they were most likely not very sound at first: and then another piece is cut off, and the roof sinks down to *E*. Now, besides the ugliness of a flat ceiling, there is more harm done here. Suppose that in this church there was a window which reached nearly as far as *B*. What is to be done with it when the roof gets down to *D* and to *E*? Why of course it must be blocked up: and many of the finest windows in the country have been spoilt in this very way. The best roofing is of lead : in former times nothing else was ever used ; but it is apt to crack with the heat. I hope you will never think of that shameful way of raising money, when you want it for the chureh, to sell the lead, and put tiles in its place."

It must be in justice remarked, that many of the high roofs were removed and lowered long before the change of religion ; and this is an additional proof, that with the introduction of the four-centered arch, and consequent departure from the verticle principle, the spirit of pointed architecture was on the wane.

The second tract refers to the state of parochial churches in large and populous towns. After noticing, in the first place, that the destruction of the ancient fabrics in such situations has not arisen from want of funds, but from the injudicious expenditure of large sums, the writer proceeds to denounce the common enormities of high pews, galleries, blocked up arches, huge stoves and pipes, plastered ceilings under oak roofs, &c. On all these matters the observations are most judicious, but as they chiefly refer to Protestant monstrosities, they are not extracted into these pages; but the following remarks on modern sepulchral monuments 'are quite applicable to the vile tablets and memorials for the dead, which are adopted by many modern Catholics in place of those appropriate and truly Catholic tombs, slabs, and brasses, which are to be found in almost every ancient church.*

"I have spoken before at much length about burials in church-yards: but I wish to say a word upon monuments. Nothing can be more unsightly than most of these, not to say irreverent and profane. You may often persuade your fellow-parishioners to give

---

* As it is very probable that many persons erect these Pagan and Protestant-looking tablets and emblems, to the memory of their departed friends, in consequence of their ignorance of ancient design, and inability to procure correct models, it may be useful to insert the following list of the various sorts of monuments anciently employed, and the average cost of executing them at the present time.

	£	£
A high tomb under a canopied arch, crotched and pinnacled, with effigy of deceased vested of natural size, angels or weepers in niches round the high tomb, with scriptures, emblems, &c. from	150	to 500
A high tomb with the effigy natural size, with weepers or tracery and shields round the sides - - - - -	50	... 100
A plain arch in a chancel, with effigy natural size - -	30	... 100
Ditto, with a slab and monumental cross and inscription -	25	... 50
A plain high tomb with inscription round edge and monumental cross on top - - - - - - - -	20	... 30
A whole length brass, under a canopy, with the evangelists in the corners, and inscription - - - - -	100	... 200
A whole length brass without canopy or evangelists - -	50	... —
A half brass with inscription and evangelists - - -	25	... 50
A ditto small - - - - - - - -	10	... 20
A quarter-size whole length effigy and inscription - -	10	... 20
A chalice with hand over in benediction, a very simple but ancient emblem of a priest's tomb - - - -	3	... 5
A brass of a cross fleury, with inscription on stem and effigy in the centre - - - - - - - -	25	... 50
A stone slab with a cross fleury, engraved in lines and inscription, shields, &c. - - - - - - - -	10	... 15
A ditto raised in Dos D'Ane, and cross fleury carved in relief on it; these are well calculated for external monuments in church-yards - - - - - - - - -	10	... 15
Stone crosses with inscriptions, to set up at the heads and feet of graves - - - - - - - -	5	... 10
Plain oak crosses with painted inscriptions for the same purpose	1	... 3

Of course the exact cost of all these different monuments will vary in proportion to quantity of detail and enrichment about them, and the materials in which they are executed; alabaster will be more costly than stone, and Purbeck marble than Yorkshire slabs, and so on; but the above lists of monuments, which are strictly in accordance with Catholic traditions, has been drawn out to show that the pious memorials used by our forefathers may be revived at the present time by all classes.

up the ugly headstones, with their vulgar doggrel rhymes, and make them choose proper emblems instead of those which are now most common. What can be worse than poppies and broken columns, which typify everlasting sleep and thwarted hopes, instead of the peaceful and hopeful rest of the Christian? But of all things shun urns: they are heathen and silly emblems, though more used perhaps than anything else. Nor are they put on monuments only: I know of more than one east end stuck about with urns and pots of different sizes and colours ; of a beautiful porch groaning under the weight of a shapeless modern urn; and even of a chancel-arch removed altogether to make way for an urn on the top of each pier. At any rate you can hinder the mutilation of the church itself for urns and monuments. It is a shame to cut away piers and carvings and mouldings, and to block up arches and windows for such things as these. It is a shame also to use monumental stones over again, and thus destroy the record of one man's life to make room for that of another. And again, it is worse than dishonest to take gravestones for one's own purposes, and even to give them away to others for doorsteps and lintels, or the like uses.

" Nothing is more strange than the modern taste in monuments: the same people who would gladly get rid of the few statues of saints and martyrs of old which have been saved for us, will themselves put up images to modern preachers, and perhaps even to wicked men, and this over the very altar itself !"

The latter part of this extract does not, of course, refer to any Catholic churches, but it is most gratifying to perceive that the members of the Establishment are at length awakened to the glaring inconsistency of permitting images of pagan divinities to be erected within their churches, while those of saints, and of our blessed Redeemer himself, are rigidly excluded.

The remarks of the writer respecting the churchyard cross, are also quite in the true spirit. He says you should care for this old cross and keep it clean, for none but wicked men would have broken the emblem of all our hopes. His conclusion is so Catholic, that it would seem to have been written ere England's unhappy schism ; indeed, such sentiments, and feelings only can belong, consistently, to the old time. May God grant that they are at least the harbingers of better days.

" And now I have done. And though I know how feebly I have raised my voice, yet it has been raised with the one view of trying to recall some of my brethren of the laity of England to a sense of what God claims from those who are entrusted here with the over-charge of His House ; and of giving what little aid to them a life devoted to Church-antiquities may have enabled me to give. If I have had much fault to find, it is not from a love of finding fault; far from that, but from a hope of amending. And if many have been persuaded by my former words to do something for God's Church, although with such scanty means, it is not much to hope that some of those to whom I now write, who mostly are so much better able to afford such cost, will also do their part. You to whom I have now been speaking are often men of wealth and influence: you have fair houses and costly furniture, and all comforts you wish for. I earnestly call upon you to think of the claims which the church, which you are allowed to watch and guard, has upon your aid: the church, within which you were by holy baptism made members of the spiritual Church; in which it may be you knelt before the bishop in confirmation, and in holy matrimony plighted your troth in the dearest earthly tie; the church which you have perhaps daily entered for prayer and praise, and how often for holy communion! around which your fathers and brethren who have departed in faith are resting in the sleep of peace; in which lastly the solemn funeral service will ere long be heard over your bier. It is no slight band which ties you to your parish-church; it is no far-off call which is rousing you to do your duty. Your oaths, your honour, your manliness, must force you, one would think, to fill the office which you have taken as a good man should: a happy office surely, to watch that church round which all your hopes are or ought to be centered; and a high office, (it cannot be too often said) to care for the holy house where God himself deigns to dwell.

"Join then for your Church's sake the zealous band who are now on all sides working each in his way for God's glory. I cannot promise you fame: but you will not desire that. I can promise you the love of all who are working in the same good cause; and, what is more, a lasting record of your labours by Him in Whose name and for Whose sake you labour."

We now come to the tract entitled *A Few Words to Church Builders,* which contains much important matter, and is certainly the first distinct publication which has issued from the present Establishment, in which ecclesiastical architecture is viewed in its true light. In the introduction, the writer remarks, that the observations "are intended for the use of those to whom God has given, not only the means, but the will, to undertake a work, *the noblest perhaps in which man can engage,* the building of a house in some degree worthy of His majesty. He farther states, that "it is his intention to dwell rather on the *Catholic* than on the *architectural* principles which ought to influence the building of a church;" and this intention constitutes the great merit, value, and, we may add, in the present day, the novelty of this publication.

The greater portion of the remarks are so excellent, and so fully illustrate the principles of church architecture, that we cannot refrain from giving copious extracts. Speaking of the dedication, the writer observes:

" 5. In a cold and faithless age like this, to attach any importance to the selection of a patron saint will probably provoke a smile in some, and in others may cause a more serious feeling of displeasure at the superstition of those who do it. We are well content, if it be so, to lie under the same charge, and for the same cause, as Andrewes, Hooker, and Whitgift. Let us give an example or two of the motives which lead to the choice of a patron saint now. In a large town in the south of England a meeting-house was built by a dissenter, who called it, out of compliment to his wife, Margaret chapel. This being afterwards bought for a church, is now named *Saint* Margaret's. In the same town is another chapel called All Souls, 'because all souls may there hear the word of God.' Other dedications are now given, which were rarely, if ever, in use among our ancestors. Such are—St. Paul, instead of SS. Peter and Paul ; Christ Church, and St. Saviour's, for a small building ; Emmanuel church, and the like. But who would found a church in England—once the 'England of Saints'—without some attention to the local memory of those holy men whose names still live in the appellations of many of our towns ? Who, in the diocese of Lichfield, would forget St. Chad ? in that of Durham, St. Cuthbert ? in those of Canterbury and Ely, St. Alphege, and St. Etheldreda ? Surely, near St. Edmund's Bury, a church-founder would naturally think of St. Edmund, or in the west of Wales, of St. David ?"

The next remark is very important, and cannot be too strongly urged to those among the English Catholics, who, having been so long confined to mere chapels, have conceived a dislike, and a most Protestant dislike it is, to chancels.

"6. There are two parts, and only two parts, which are absolutely essential to a church—chancel and nave. If it have not the latter, it is at best only a chapel ; if it have not the former, it is little better than a meeting-house. The twelve thousand ancient churches in this land, in whatever else they may differ, agree in this, that every one has or had a well-defined chancel. On the least symbolical grounds, it has always been felt right to separate off from the rest of the church a portion which should be expressly appropriated to the more solemn rites of our religion ; and this portion is the chancel. In this division our ancient architects recognised an emblem of the holy Catholic Church ; as this consists of two parts, the Church militant and the Church triumphant, so does the earthly structure also consist of two parts, the chancel and nave ; the Church militant being typified by the latter, and the

The material originally positioned here is too large for reproduction in this reissue. A PDF can be downloaded from the web address given on page iv of this book, by clicking on 'Resources Available'.

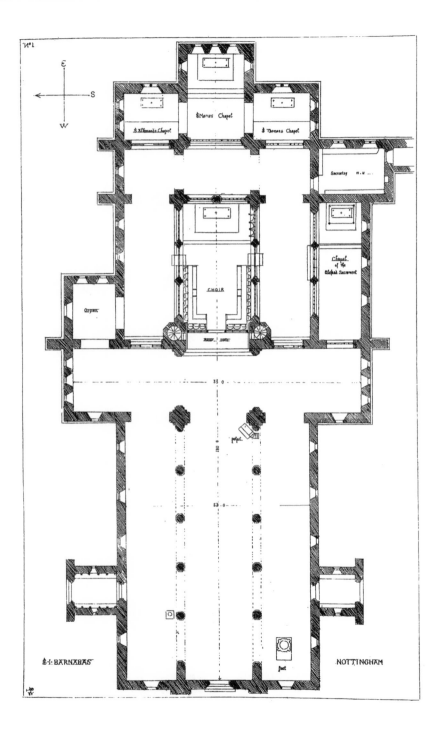

N°1.

E
←—— S
W

S¹ Maries Chapel

S¹ Alfreunds Chapel   S¹ Thomas Chapel

Sacristy N · E ...

Chapel
of the
Blessed Sacrament

Organ

CHOIR

CHOIR STEP

35 0

pulpit

180 0

53 0

font

S·¹· BARNABAS   NOTTINGHAM

Church triumphant by the former. But in nine-tenths of 'new churches,' we shall find no attempt whatever at having a distinct chancel, or it is at best confined to a small apsidal projection of the altar. And this, one of the most glaring faults of modern buildings, has not met with the reprobation which it so well deserves; nay, has even been connived at by those who knew better. To illustrate the respective sizes of ancient and modern chancels, I subjoin [Plate 2] two ground plans, one of a church built about 1250, the other of one within a mile of it, erected in 1835. And surely, if we had no other reason for the prominence we attach to a chancel than that without one exception our ancestors attached such prominence to it, it ought to be enough for us who profess to admire their wisdom, and as far as we may, to tread in their steps."

In the new Catholic churches of Southport, Keighley, Kenilworth, St. Oswald's, near Liverpool, Macclesfield, Dudley, Pomfret, Masborough, St. George's, London, &c., the chancels are built precisely after the ancient models, and bear a good relative proportion to the length of the church; they are also duly provided with screens, sedilia, sepulchres, reredoses, &c.

"7. This division, essential in the interior, is not always to be traced in the exterior. It is far better indeed, generally speaking, that it should be marked in both; and to this end the breadth of the chancel should be a little less than that of the nave; a difference of four or five feet will be quite sufficient. The height of the chancel is usually less, in the same proportion. Sometimes this latter is the only mark of division, as in the churches of Chailey and Southease, Sussex. In a cross church, it will be sufficiently marked by the transepts. The only kind of church in which it cannot be externally shewn, is where there are chancel and nave, with two aisles to both; but this is rarely the case, except in city churches, or where the builders were cramped for room."

This is frequently to be remarked in those churches built in crowded cities, and in some of the larger parish churches, such as Newark, &c. where most probably this arrangement was adopted for the purpose of obtaining a Lady chapel beyond the high altar. The annexed plate, No. 1, will show the ground-plan of the Catholic church of St. Barnabas, now erecting at Nottingham, where the chancel is entirely surrounded by aisles and eastern chapels.* In the church of St.

---

* We introduce three engravings (Nos. 1, 2, 3) to illustrate the design of this church, which when complete will be the most perfect revival of a large parochial church that has been yet accomplished. Beneath the choir is a crypt, with vaulting springing from two rows of low pillars; at the eastern end of this undercroft is an altar dedicated in honour of St. Peter, as being the foundation or rock of the church. The same staircases which lead up to the rood loft, at the entrance of the choir, are continued down to the crypt, which is lit by the

Andrew, about to be erected at Cambridge, the space being exceedingly limited, the chancel is taken out of the east compartment enclosed by open screen work, with an aisle on each side. The writer then states, respecting cruciform churches:

"9. A cross is of course the most beautiful form in which a church can be built. Yet those persons who think it necessary to a perfect building, are in great error; not one-tenth of the churches in the country having been erected in that shape. From this mistaken idea transepts have been attempted with funds hardly sufficient for chancel and nave, often to the destruction of the fair proportion of the chancel. The symbol conveyed by the cross is certainly better adapted than any other for a Christian place of worship; yet that of a ship, which the other form sets forth, is by no means unsuitable, and was a very favourite one with the early Church, as St. Chrysostom and St. Hilary (writing concerning the Saviour's walking on the sea) testify. A very general fault of modern cross churches is the excessive breadth of each of the four arms; whence the arches to the lantern, or central part of the

---

side openings in the walls of the choir, which being elevated several feet above the pavement of the aisles, afford sufficient space for their introduction. The various chapels, as well as the choir, will be enclosed by oak screens of open tracery and panel work, relieved in colours. That portion of the church eastward of the transept, will be divided off from the rest of the building by open screens and gates on a line with the great roodscreen. The roodloft will extend the whole width between the great east pillars supporting the tower, and raised about fourteen feet from the level of the choir; in breadth it will be about seven feet, and in the centre a great rood will be erected, with appropriate images, standards for lights, &c.

The choir will be furnished with eighteen carved oak stalls and desks, precisely on the old model; and at the back of the stalls are oak screens, which will extend along both sides of the choir between the pillars. The pavement of the choir and sanctuary, as well as that of the eastern chapels, will consist of incrusted tiles of various colours, similar in design and composition to those used in ancient churches. On the epistle side of the altar will be fixed the sedilia, framed and carved in wood, similar in design to those still remaining in the choir of Westminster, and vulgarly called King Sebert's tomb. The high altar will consist of a single slab of stone, supported on eight shafts of Petworth marble, with gilt cap and bases. Immediately behind the altar a rich perforated oak screen will extend across the eastern extremity of the choir, enriched with gold and colours, and surmounted by standards for wax tapers. Through this screen the arched entrance and stained windows of the Lady chapel will be distinctly seen. In a chapel on the epistle or south side of the choir, the blessed sacrament will be reserved, on a rich altar surmounted by a ciborium, or canopy, supported on four gilt pillars, between which curtains will run on brass rods, extending from cap to cap. The windows of this church are all intended to be glazed with stained glass, of various devices and subjects, in the rich early style; and it is proposed eventually to cover all the spandrils of the arches, walls, &c., with painted enrichments. The organ will be placed in the north transept. All the altars will be furnished with candlesticks, sacred vessels, hangings, and other ornaments in the same character as the building; and to the minutest details this church will be a strict revival of Catholic antiquity.

cross, are made obtuse to an almost absurd degre ; and sometimes are omitted altogether, as unnecessary. But if they are unnecessary to the safety of a church, they suggest (according to the great authority on such points, Durandus) an important symbolical meaning ; namely, that by the writings of the four Evangelists the doctrine of the cross has been preached through the whole world. And this is the reason that we so often find the Evangelistic symbols on, or over them."

We most heartily concur with these remarks; cruciform churches should not be attempted, unless the transepts are well prolonged, and they should always be accompanied by a central tower, or four solid stone arches prepared to receive one, and the chancel should be *at least* the depth of one of the transepts. A transept church built in the form of a T, without a chancel, is quite irregular. The evangelistic symbols are found on the extremities of crosses at a very early period, and may be considered indispensable to a rood cross. They are found on the earliest known examples of processional crosses, and were also engraven on, or affixed to, the silver covers of the holy Gospels. The abbey barn at Glastonbury is cruciform, and a most noble structure; in each gable is a quatrefoil with an emblem of an Evangelist, and the same is to be occasionally observed on cross-built churches.

The following remark shows that the writer is fully imbued with the feelings and spirit of the ancient architects.

" 11. There is not the slightest objection, whatever the fastidious taste of modern times may think of it, against building at first one aisle, if the funds are not sufficient for the erection of two. And it is far more in accordance with Catholic principles to build one aisle as it ought to be, than to 'run up' two cheaply ; always supposing it in this, as in other cases of imperfect design, to be the intention of the builder, that the church shall, at some future time, though perhaps not by himself, be completed. And this leads to an important remark. It is not of consequence that the opposite sides of a church should correspond with each other. Churches with one aisle, or one transept, constantly occur. I will prove this by some examples, taken at random :—Llanfwrog, Denbighshire, has N. aisle ; Tal-y-Llyn, Merion, S. transept ; Brandon, Suffolk, S. aisle ; Avening, Gloucestershire, N. aisle ; Rodborough, Gloucestershire, N. aisle to chancel and nave, and S. transept ; Hunsdon, Herts, S. transept ; Stanford, Berks, N. aisle ; Erith, Kent, S. aisle to chancel and nave.

" But now, in most people's opinion, the great beauty of a church, if it have two aisles, consists in having both sides the same in details ; whereas nothing can be more opposite to the true principles

E

of ecclesiastical architecture than this idea, so cramping to boldness of design and variety of ornament.

"12. This remark applies particularly to the position of the tower. Now-a-days, it is almost universally placed at the west end of the church, that it may 'stand in the middle;' whereas the following positions are equally good : the intersection of a cross church, or between the chancel and nave, where the church is not cross ; these are very common. Other positions are :—Middle of north aisle, Vaucelles, near Caen ; middle of nave, Caen, S. Sauveur ; North of chancel, Berneval, Normandy ; South of chancel, Standon, Hertfordshire ; North end of the north transept, Montgomery ; South end of the south transept, East Lavant, Sussex ; North side of the nave, Goustranville, near Caen ; South side of the nave, Midhurst, Sussex ; East end of the north aisle, Patching, Sussex ; West end of the north aisle, Clapham, Sussex ; East end of the south aisle, West Grinstead, Sussex ; West end of the south aisle, Amiens, S. Loup ; Holyrood, Southampton ; North-west angle of nave, York, St. Crux ; South-west angle of nave, Sacombe, Herts ; Western part of the chancel, Yainville, Normandy. It shows the perverseness of modern times, that the only position in which a tower never ought to be built, namely over the altar, is almost the only one which in modern churches ever takes place of that at the west end ; and it is adopted for the same reason,—it is 'just in the middle,' too."

Now we could embrace the man who wrote this; for the senseless uniformity of modern design is one of its greatest defects. The idea of everything being exactly alike on both sides, has created an unreal style of building which was quite unknown to our ancestors, and it is most delightful to see the very soul of modern deformities thus ably attacked. When once the trammels and bondage of this regularity system are broken through, and people are taught not to consider a portico and two uniform wings the perfection of design, we may expect vast improvements ; and we hail with the greatest satisfaction this champion of true principles, who at once proclaims defiance to the pagan and mock-regularity men, and sets forth a speedy return to the real and consistent manner of building practised in the days of faith.

We pass over in this place the writer's remarks respecting altars and sedilia, as they contain serious errors and mistatements, which will be noticed in full hereafter, and proceed to the subject of fonts, of which he observes :

"28. The subject of Fonts is highly interesting ; a list of models will be given in the Appendix. The reader cannot do better than consult Mr. Poole's before-mentioned little work, where he will find much valuable information on the subject. To his remarks there we may add a few more.

" The shape of the bason may be either square, circular, or octagonal ; the greater number of examples in each style are octagonal ; an octagon being a very ancient symbol of regeneration. Where there is a central, and four corner shafts, the latter have capital and base ; the former has neither. Hexagonal fonts, though they do occur, are not to be imitated ; yet they are not always late ; that at Ramsey, which is Norman, is of this shape. A pentagonal font, of which Mr. Poole has not an example, occurs at Hollington, Sussex ; a heptagonal one at Chaddesden, Derbyshire. I quite agree with Mr. Poole, that coats of arms are to be avoided in ornamenting the instrument of our initiation into Him, who 'was despised and rejected of men.' Yet shields do occur in early fonts : for example, at West Deeping, Lincolnshire, which is early English. And shields, with the instruments of crucifixion, and the like, would be no less beautiful than appropriate ornaments.

" A kneeling-stone at the west side appears desirable ; it may be panelled to any degree of richness. It need hardly be observed that the cover should be richly carved in oak ; there is a magnificent specimen in Castle Acre, Norfolk, about sixteen feet in height. The pulley, by which it is elevated, is sometimes, as in Stamford S. George, curiously carved ; the Fall of Man, the Baptism of our Saviour, and His victory over the devil, are here frequently represented.

" The position of the font *must be in the nave, and near a door ;* this cannot be too much insisted on : it thus typifies the admission of a child into the Church by Holy Baptism. The Canon orders that it shall stand in the ancient usual place ; and I quote the following passages from the Visitation Articles of some of the prelates before-mentioned."

The Rev. G. A. Poole's remarks, to which the writer alludes, are as follows:

" Having well entered the church, the first object that claims our attention is the font, which always is or ought to be placed at the west end, near the principal entrance, to symbolize the great truth, that holy baptism, of which the font is the instrument, is the sacrament of admission into the Christian church. Great varieties of form and arrangement are found in fonts, all appropriate, and many of them exquisite both in design and in execution : for the earlier ecclesiastics of this kingdom, like those who truly represent the Anglican Church at the present day, held holy baptism as the great sacrament of a high mystery and privilege, and accordingly lavished on the font the greatest possible care and art. Nor is there any part of the church, or of its furniture, which has been so often preserved through all the successive changes which have taken place in the surrounding buildings, as the font. Hence we have many more Norman fonts than Norman churches; and it is probable that several fonts now existing in buildings of comparatively recent date are among the very oldest relics of ancient ecclesiastic architecture.

"One thing is to be observed in all those fonts which deserve the slightest notice, and it is one which ought on no account whatever to be forgotten at the present day:—that they are all sufficiently large to baptize children by immersion. This is the rule, however many may be the exceptions, and however accounted for, of the Church of England : and it is equally irreverent, absurd, and inconsistent, to substitute a small basin, as is now too often done, for a deep and broad font.

"But to proceed to some of the forms and ornaments of fonts,— and to arrange them, nearly at least, in a chronological order :—

"If rudeness be taken as an indication of antiquity, the first place must be given to some which are little more than large stones, scarcely reduced to any definite shape, except near the top, and then hollowed sufficiently for the purpose for which they are designed. Among these may be mentioned the font of Little Maplestead, one of the round churches already mentioned,* and that at Heron Gate, in Essex.†

"The first well-defined shape which the font assumes, seems to be that of a circular tub-shaped vessel, with little grace of form, except that which arises from the base being somewhat smaller than the rim. At St. Martin's church, Canterbury,‡ is a font in which this proportion is inverted, and the effect is certainly less pleasing. Some of these round, tub-shaped fonts may be of Saxon, many of them are certainly of Norman date. Simple as this form is, it is frequently very graceful; and when adorned with a series of arches and pillars in relief, with § or without figures under each arch, and elevated on a step, or it may be three steps, a font of this figure is no unworthy occupant of the west end of a Norman church.

"Somewhat later came the square stone, hollowed in the centre, and supported by a single massive column,‖ to which it forms a capital; or on one large central, and four smaller columns.¶ This arrangement obviously affords greater room for the symbolical figures of the ecclesiastical designer, on the four large flat sides; and, accordingly, they were often adorned in this way profusely and most ingeniously. Perhaps the most frequent decorations of such fonts as these are emblematical representations of the fall of man; which is the part of scripture history best adapted to the entrance

---

* Britton's Architectural Antiq., vol. i.   † Antiquarian Itinerary, vol. vii.
‡ Britton's Architectural Antiq., vol. v.   § As at Avington, ibid.
‖ As at Castle Rising, Norfolk, ibid.
¶ As at East Meon and Winchester (ibid.); and at Iffley, Oxfordshire (Glossary of Architecture), and several other places.

of our churches, and admirably placed on the font, in which is washed away the stain which thence descends upon all the descendants of Adam. By way of specimen, I will enumerate the figures which occupy the two carved sides of the font of East Meon church, Hampshire.*

"The first group represents the creation of Adam, and the formation of Eve from his side. Then we have Adam and Eve standing on either side of the tree of the knowledge of good and evil, near which is the serpent speaking to them. Eve appears eating, and Adam just gathering the fruit. These occupy the first side ; and opposite we have the expulsion of the guilty pair from paradise, which is represented by the angel with a drawn sword driving them from a magnificent palace. Afterwards another angel appears with a spade, from whom Adam is anxiously receiving instruction in husbandry ; while Eve, who like her husband now appears in the garment provided for them by the goodness of God, is diligently occupied with her distaff. The whole design and execution of these several figures is extremely rude, and even grotesque ; but nothing can be more transparent than the meaning of the whole, which is the principal object : and the appropriateness of the design in that place is obvious. The font of Winchester cathedral † is extremely like that just described in general character ; but the design of the sculpture is different, and instead of being easily understood, is so obscure as not yet to have been certainly deciphered. We have, however, a symbol which we should, *a priori*, expect on a Christian font, and which was, indeed, one of the first which in the primitive churches was introduced into the baptistery,—I mean the dove, an emblem of the third person in the ever blessed and glorious Trinity, by whom we are regenerated in the water of baptism. A salamander also appears on this font, in allusion to the words which St. John spake of our blessed Lord, ' He shall baptize you with the Holy Ghost and with fire.'‡

The font of Burnham Deepdale,§ in Norfolk, affords a series of designs, of which the subject is very clear, but the appropriateness to the place where they appear not so obvious. Twelve compartments are filled with as many representations of the different labours of the husbandman. Is not this a translation, so to speak, into the vernacular tongue, of the processes of the vineyard, by which the good works of Christians were symbolized in Italy and other vine countries ? Their vintage and our harvest may symbolize the same moral precepts and religious truths ; and this font of Burnham Deepdal reads the same lesson with the baptistery of

---

* Archæologia, x.
+ Winkle's Cathedrals.   Britton's Arch. Antiq., vol. v.
‡ Matthew, iii. 2.   The salamander also appears over a representation of our blessed Lord's baptism, in the very rude square font at Bridekirk.
§ Archæologia, x. 189.

Constantine, near St. Agnese, in Rome, on the ceiling of which are represented in mosaic the processes of the vintage.*

Many other variations of square fonts might be mentioned, and many remarkable decorations might be adduced ; but I pass on to more important changes in the form of the font. A font of five sides I do not know to occur any where ; and hexagonal fonts, though not rare, are less common than either round, square, or octagonal ones. That at Carlisle Cathedral is hexagonal ; and so is that at Farringdon, in Berkshire. Bredon font, Worcestershire, is also hexagonal, and adorned on each face with an escutcheon, charged with arms ;† and I especially note this ornament in connexion with an hexagonal font, because I think the form and the ornament equally unecclesiastical and barbarous. I can imagine no reason either of symbolical meaning, or of beauty to the eye,‡ which can plead for a six-sided figure, in preference to a circle, a square, or an octagon : and as for the ensigns of worldly pomp, and of human pride, on the instruments of initiation into the Church of Christ, into the mystical body of Him who was 'despised and rejected of men,' I cannot see any congruity in it at all. And it is worthy of remark, that this inapposite decoration for the font, if decoration it can be called, came into use just when heraldry had lost whatever religion it once had. So long as it was in any sense religious, it was too humble to appear in such a place ; but after the conclusion of the Crusades, and with the mock chivalry of the Tudors, with hexagon fonts and debased architecture, first appeared the custom of decorating fonts with armorial bearings.§

The custom, however, thus introduced, did not cease until it had deformed many much later fonts ; for instance, the somewhat in-

---

* Hope's Essay on Architecture.

† Which are as follows :—1. A chevron between three garbs. 2. A chevron between three spread eagles. 3 and 5. Seven mascles conjoined, 3, 3, 1. 6. A bend. See Archæologia, x. p. 194.

‡ The hexagon is, perhaps, the least beautiful of all regular figures when seen singly, but the most beautiful in combination. Indeed, it is, as if by mathematical skill, adapted for close compact: for it is the figure which in composition will enclose the largest space within the smallest circumference, without any intervening spaces. The arrangement of the cells in a honeycomb will exemplify what I mean. Had the cells been triangular or quadrangular, the quantity of wax employed in their walls would have been greater in proportion to their size; had they been any other figures except hexagons, there would have been spaces between them.

§ I mean that the escutcheon was not introduced till then as the mere receptacle of armorial bearings: when the shield was introduced as a part of the costume of the figures with which the font was adorned, it was probably enough charged with arms. Such figures with shields appear on the font of Wansford, Northamptonshire, figured in the Archæologia, xvi. plate xxxvii., and referred by Mr. Repton (see p. 195) to the eleventh and twelfth century. Even angels are represented in this way bearing blazoned shields, as in one of the bosses in the south transept of York Minster.

elegant octagonal font at Sefton,* (Lancashire,) and the decidedly inelegant font, also octagonal, at South Kilvington, Yorkshire. The latter is figured in the sixteenth volume of the Archæologia, and affords the materials, from its eight escutcheons, of a pedigree of the Scropes.

"I know of but one font whose basin has seven sides.   It is at Elmeswell, in Suffolk,† that also is cumbered with armorial bearings.

" And now we arrive at the octagon, the most appropriate form for the font, and the most beautiful as well as the most ecclesiastical ; for the octagon is not only a very graceful form, and very favourable to the reception of sculpture on its several faces, but it is also in itself symbolical, according to the ancient method of spiritualising numbers, of the new birth in Baptism : for the seven days' creation of the natural world are symbolised by the number seven ; and the new creation by Christ Jesus, by the number eight, in allusion to the eighth day, on which he rose again from the dead. And this reason St. Ambrose, more than fourteen centuries ago, assigned for the octagonal form of the Baptistery :

' Octachorum sanctos templum surrexit in usus,
          Octagonus fons est, munere dignus eo.
     Hoc numero decuit sacri baptismatis aulam
          Surgere, quo populis vera salus rediit
     Luce resurgentis Christi, qui claustra resolvit
          Mortis, et a tumulis, suscitet examines.'‡

" A few of the more remarkable fonts of this figure may be noted.

" That at Ware, in Hertfordshire, is charged with whole length figures, in very bold relief, of the salutation of St. John the Baptist, of St. James the less, of St. Catherine, of St. George, of St. Christopher, and of St. Margaret, and the dragon.   Between the compartments, busts of angels hold musical instruments, and the instruments of the Passion.§   The font at St. Martin's, Oxford, is figured in the glossary of architecture ; it is richly adorned with quatrefoils, niches, and statues.   The fonts of St. Mary Magdalen's, and of St. Aldate's, Oxford, are given in the same work : the former of these has the merit of being an example of the decorated style, in which but few fonts are remaining.   The last is much later, about A. D. 1520.‖

" But by far the most graceful and splendid form of the font is the octagonal basin elevated on a shaft or column, rising out of

---

* Figured in the antiquities of Sefton church, by R. Bridgens.
† Archæologia, x. 194. I am now able to add that of Bowden Magna Leicestershire.
‡ These lines were formerly inscribed over the font of S. Tecla.
§ Figured in the Antiquarian Itinerary, vol. i.
‖ These three fonts are also figured in the memorials of Oxford.

several steps ; the shaft and basin (and sometimes even the steps), being richly adorned with panels or niches, with statues or groups of figures, and in short, with all the decorations which their style of architecture admits. Fonts of this character may interest us the more, because they are such as ought to be erected in the greater number of new churches, being adapted to the style of architecture, (or to whatever there is of architectural style), now generally affected. An extremely graceful font of this character is that of Worsted, in Norfolk ;* it is without statues, (though there may have been small figures once in the niches of the shaft) but is richly decorated with quatrefoils and flowing tracery. It is not too elaborate to be easily imitated, nor too rich for an ordinary parish church.

"The grace and elegance of this form rises to magnificence, when the niches and compartments are occupied with statues and groups, as in the font of East Dereham, in Norfolk ; which was erected in 1468. The several items of expenditure in its erection, with the manner in which the sum was collected, still remain as a subject of curiosity. The account is too long to repeat. The last font that I shall mention is also the most beautiful. It is that at Walsingham in Norfolk, and is thus described by Britton, who gives also a beautiful plate of it in his Ecclesiastical Antiquities.† 'It is decorated,' he says, 'with all the charms of art ; with all the blandishments of sculpture and architecture.‡ When first raised it must have excited admiration, bordering on enthusiastic devotion. The whole consists of three portions, or divisions in height ; a base or steps, a shaft, and a capital or basin. In the first are two tiers, or series of steps, raised above the pavement, each of which is ornamented on the exterior face with various panels and tracery. Each is also subdivided into two steps : the upper step, or surface, is formed by two divisions in its elevation, and eight in its horizontal plane. From the centre of this rises the shaft, which is surrounded by canopied niches, pinnacles, buttresses, pediments, and statues. At the angles are eight smaller statues standing on pedestals, and a series of trefoil lees extends round the upper member of this shaft, which is surmounted by the basin or font. This consists, like all other parts, of eight faces, each of which displays a canopied recess filled with a group of figures in basso relievo, representing the seven sacraments, with the crucifixion :

---

* Archæologia, xvi. 336.   † Vol. iv. p. 108.

‡ He adds, " and Catholic superstition :" but as I am at a loss to discover any superstition in the represantation of certain ceremonies which are surely religious, and which not the sculptor but the person who describes his work calls sacraments, and which in a lower sense than that in which we polemically use the word might safely be called sacraments, I have omitted the word *superstition* in this quotation.

I. Baptism. II. Confirmation. III. Penance. IV. The Eucharist. V. Ordination. VI. Marriage. VII. Extreme Unction."

We have given these observations at full length, as they are decidedly the best remarks on the form and decoration of this *most important* and, we may add, *now most neglected* piece of church furniture, that have yet appeared. Indeed, the lectures themselves are well deserving the most attentive perusal, and were it not for certain most inconsistent expressions, they would be worthy of a Catholic ecclesiastic.

But to return to the Camdenians. In the twenty-ninth division, the restoration of ancient glazed and figured tile pavement is advocated; and truly, unless these be revived, our churches will never produce the rich and harmonious effect of the ancient ones. The specimens now remaining of these ornamented tile floors are in general so worn and mutilated, that they convey but a very imperfect idea of their pristine beauty to a general observer; but their effect on a grand scale, as in the chapter-houses of Salisbury, Westminster, or York, must have been truly splendid; their manufacture has been lately most successfully revived in the Potteries. The chancel of the conventual chapel at Birmingham, and that of St. John's Hospital, Alton, have already been laid after the ancient manner with great effect; and it is proposed to lay the whole floor of St. Giles's church, now erecting at Cheadle, and all the chapels and choirs of St. Barnabas, Nottingham, in a similar manner. The present cost of these pavements, exclusive of the original moulds and the laying down, is sixpence per tile, or eighteen shillings the square yard, and an increased demand would of course have the effect of reducing the expense in proportion. In churches where much gilding and colour is introduced, these incrusted tiles of various hues are indispensable to produce harmony of effect; for if so large a surface as the pavement is left of a dull uniform tint, whilst the rest of the building is covered with diaper and ornament, the contrast will be painfully striking. To remedy this defect, most modern sanctuaries are covered with drugget or carpeting, but these always produce a chamberlike appearance, and soon become faded and shabby, while enameled tiles far exceed them in richness of appearance, do not suffer any deterioration from damp, and impart a distinctive ecclesiastical character; of course their introduction does not preclude carpeting from being laid on the altar steps, &c. during the celebration of mass. Coopertoria are frequently mentioned in old church inventories,* but these should be wove in appropriate designs, and as dissimilar as possible to those in ordinary domestic use.

The next important remark is relative to roodscreens.

" 35. We have seen that the chancel and nave are to be kept entirely separate. This is done by the roodscreen, that most beautiful and Catholic appendage to a church. We have also seen that the prelates of the seventeenth century required it as a necessary ornament; and that they who were most inveterate against rood-lofts always held the roodscreen sacred. Why is it that *not one* modern church has it? It constitutes one of the peculiar beauties of English buildings; for abroad it is very rare. There can be no objection to the erection of a perpendicular screen in a church of earlier style; because such was the constant practice, and because that style is better adapted for woodwork than any other. The whole may, and indeed ought to be, richly painted and gilded. The lower part, which is not pierced, may be painted with figures of saints, as in Castle Acre, Norfolk; Therfield, Hertfordshire; Guilden Morden, Cambridgeshire; Bradninch, Devonshire; why S. Edmund the King so often occurs is not known. In the appendix, nothing will be given but what might well serve as a model, though some instances may be much mutilated."

As many English Catholics of the present time, through ignorance of the antiquity and use of these divisions between the clergy and people, entertain most extraordinary, and, we may add, uncatholic prejudices and objections against their revival, it seems proper to enter upon this important subject at some length.

Roodscreens and lofts are not to be regarded as mere architectural enrichments raised for effect, nor as enclosures for the sole purpose of protecting the chancel from improper intrusion; for although they contribute to both these ends, yet their real intention must be sought for on profound mystical reasons. Father Thiers has divided his learned treatise on

---

* " Cathedral Church of York. Coopertoria.
" Item, one large carpet to lay before the high altar on festivals.
" Item, a small carpet.
" Item, two large carpets to lay on the steps of the high altar, one of which has garbs, the other the arms of the Lord Scrope, lined with canvass.
" Item, a white carpet with double roses.
" Item, three blue carpets, with the arms of N. John Pakenham, late treasurer."—*Dugdale's Monasticon.*
" Item, ten cloths, called pede cloths, to lye before the high altar in the Ladye's chapel.
" Item, four pede cloaths, called tapets."—*Gunton's Hist. of the Church of Peterburgh.*

roodlofts into thirty-four chapters, containing a most elaborate account of their origin and purpose. As this treatise is a good-sized volume in itself, it is only possible to glance at the leading portions of the work, but these will be amply sufficient to set forth their real use and importance. The great intention of these screens and lofts is twofold.

1. To mark the separation between the faithful and the sacrifice, the nave and chancel, emblematic of the Church militant and the Church triumphant, into which latter we can alone enter by the merits of Christ's passion on the cross, whose image, as crucified for our sins, is affixed on high above the centre of the screen.

2. To enable the deacon to chaunt the holy Gospel to the faithful from a high place, in accordance with the practice and tradition of the Church in all ages. This custom is attested by most of the ecclesiastical writers of antiquity, and it was preserved in many of the French cathedrals down to the time of the great revolution of 1790. So that the roodlofts might have been called with propriety, the throne of the Word of God.*

---

* "Cathedral de St. Jean de Lyon.—Le diacre demande la bénédiction au célébrant; et ils vont au jubé en cet ordre. Le portemasse, les deux portechandeliers, le soudiacre d'office tenant un coussin devant sa poitrine, un des diacres assistans tenant l'encensoir, puis le diacre tenant les livres des évangiles que personne lorsqu'il passe ne salue, *ils montent au jubé;* là le soudiacre regarde le diacre en face, puis après ces mots, 'sequentia sancti evangelii secundum,' le diacre se tourne avec tout le chœur vers l'autel et fait comme le célébrant un triple signe de croix. On n'encense point le livre ni avant ni après, *mais seulement le grand crucifix du jubé* est encensé de trois coups avant l'évangile et trois coups après.

"St. Maurice D'Angers.—Le grand diacre ayant commencé l'ante évangelium, l'orgue la continue, et cependant on va au jubé en cet ordre. En allant deux thuriféraires parfument d'encens le chemin de chaque côté, suivis de deux portechandeliers, puis un petit diacre portant le texte des épîtres, et le grand diacre celui des évangiles, vont tous trois par le côté de l'épître et *montent au jubé,* &c.

"St. Etienne D'Auxerre.—Le diacre va au jubé lire l'évangile, étant précédé d'un enfant de chœur qui porte une voile environ de deux pieds et demi pour couvrir le pupître, sur lequel l'évangile doit être chanté, des deux portechandeliers et du portecroix; puis marchent le thuriféraire, le soudiacre, et le diacre portant le livre des évangiles fort haut: *ils montent en cet ordre au jubé,*" etc.

De Moleon, Voyage Liturgique.

These are only a few of the many instances cited in the above work, to prove that the original use of the roodlofts continued in many of the French Churches till the great revolution.

The "Voyage Liturgique" is a most edifying work, and gives an impressive account of the great solemnity with which the Church celebrated her sacred offices; one page of this book should be quite sufficient to silence the boastings of certain writers of these days, who, with only a bason and a pair of *unlighted candles,* talk about Catholic rites and ceremonies, and that with an authoritative tone which is as unseemly as it is ridiculous.

3. The roodlofts were generally used for preaching, both in the Eastern and Western Churches, previous to the introduction of pulpits, which are not older than the 13th century.

4. The martyrology and lessons were read from the roodlofts.

5. The festivals and fasts were announced to the faithful from the roodlofts.

6. According to a homily of St. John of Chrysostom, the deacon stood in the roodloft to pronounce those awful words *Sancta Sanctis*, to the people, before the communion.

7. The emperors were crowned in the jubé or roodloft of the great church at Constantinople, and the French kings, down to Charles the Tenth, were always enthroned in the roodloft at Rheims cathedral.

8. Antiphons, responds, versicles, and certain prayers, were chaunted from the roodlofts, as also the gradual, Alleluia, and tract.

9. The prophecies preceding the epistles on the Christmas masses, at midnight, break of day, and morning, were chanted from the rood, also the passion of our Lord on Palm Sunday and Good Friday.

These screens were to be found anciently in the greater part of the continental churches, or at least a beam, with the rood and an elevated ambo for the lecture of the Gospel.

In England, every church, previous to the great schism, was provided with a screen and roodloft. It is impossible to say the precise period when these were introduced; many of the Norman and early chancels communicating only by a small archway with the nave, the wall itself became a sort of screen, but there is little doubt that the archway was provided with gates and a rood-beam. Those in the cathedral, conventual, and collegiate churches, were generally built solid of stone, enameled with canopied niches and images, and provided with two staircases for the gospeller and epistler to ascend different ways,* on their proper sides of the choir.

---

* In the noble but shamefully neglected church of Tattershall, Lincolnshire, formerly collegiate, is a splendid roodloft of stone, with recesses for an altar on either side of the choir door; the parapet on the eastern side is corbelled out like a pulpit, for the lector, and provided with desks or ledges for books, excellently devised in the stone work. It is quite lamentable to behold this noble fabric falling to utter ruin; it must have been a sumptuous building in its glory, filled with admirable glass, elaborate carvings, and exquisite monumental brasses, now torn up and lying about, many large fragments and plates being totally lost. To this church was annexed fair collegiate buildings, with cloisters, gardens, orchards, &c.; and the establishment consisted of a master, six

In parochial churches, the screens and lofts were generally constructed of timber, and, with few exceptions, had only one staircase, usually built in a small turret outside the walls,* or in the substance of a large pillar. In this country, owing to the Protestant plan of converting the cathedral choirs into preaching places and pewing them, most of the ancient rood-lofts have escaped destruction,† and in this respect our cathedrals are far more perfect than the continental churches, where the partial decay of the ancient solemn discipline, combined with pagan ideas of taste and the ravages of the great revolution, have left but few of the sumptuous rood-lofts which were formerly to be found in every great church.‡

The roodlofts in ancient days were splendidly adorned on great festivals with lights and branches: that of All Hallow's,

---

chaplains, six clerks, six choristers, and fourteen poor brethren, till the suppression, by that sacrilegious tyrant Henry, who granted it to the then Duke of Suffolk.

* Fine examples at Lavenham church, Suffolk; St. Martin's church, Stamford, Lincolnshire; Wells church, Norfolk; Long Melford church, Suffolk; and many others.

† York, Lincoln, Exeter, (Norwich, till the late repairs,) Wells, Canterbury, Bristol, Southwell minster, Ripon minster, Christchurch, Hampshire, have all most splendid stone roodlofts, well preserved, but now used as mere organ lofts, nor have any of the ancient rites been performed in them since the schism of the English Church.

‡ The ancient roodloft of the splendid abbey of St. Ouen, Rouen, engraved in Dom Pomeraye's history of that great house, must have been truly glorious. It was provided with two circular stone staircases on either side; towards the nave it was subdivided into three grand arches, like a cloister; in the centre bay was the choir door, with brass gates of intricate design; in the other bays were two altars with reredoses, enriched with niches, canopies, and images; over the centre bay was the great rood, upwards of sixty feet high from the pavement, with images of our blessed Lady and St. John; and immediately below the base of the cross, on a corbel pedestal, an image of our blessed Lady, called of pity, with the body of our Lord. This splendid monument of Catholic piety and art, sumptuously adorned with painting, gilding, and rich furniture, was greatly injured and defaced by the French Calvinists in 1562, and finally destroyed in the revolution of 1791.

The cathedral of Alby yet possesses a splendid roodloft, of the same style as that formerly at St. Ouen.

At Louvain is a fine roodloft, with a most elaborate cross, painted and gilt in the original colours. A few years since, however, the wretched innovators removed the altars, which stood in arched recesses on each side of the choir door, and thus destroyed the lower part of this splendid screen, which now appears naked and unfinished: the same destructives would have demolished the stone tabernacle for the reservation of the blessed sacrament, because it *stood on one side of the choir*, but in this project they were happily defeated.

Although it is now exceeding rare to find roodscreens in the country parish churches on the continent, they are frequently mentioned in old documents, and there can be no doubt that they were as common as in England. It is quite a mistake to suppose that roods and roodlofts were confined to this country, —they were universal during the good time.

Bread-street, in London, was sometimes lit up with twenty-two tapers, weighing 67 lbs.* The rood and beam lights are frequently mentioned in old church accounts, and pious souls left both lands and houses to maintain these bright emblems of our Lord's glory. Coronas, or circles of light, were often suspended in the roodlofts, as at St. Jean of Lyon, where three crowns with tapers were lit on all doubles. The crosses standing in the loft were richly floreated, and ornamented with emblems of the evangelists at the extremities; and *these in very early times,* Father Thiers says, " Codin temoigne qu'il y avoit une croix d'or qui prezoit cent livres, et qui *toute eclairée de flambeaux,* et toute parsemée de pierreries au dessus du jubé de Sainte Sophie."

The great rood was certainly one of the most impressive features of a Catholic Church; and a screen surmounted with its lights and images, covered with gold and paintings of holy men, forms indeed a glorious entrance to the holy place set apart for sacrifice. We have here introduced an etching of the great screen and rood lately erected in the Cathedral Church of St. Chad, Birmingham (plate IV), and which will afford a tolerable idea of the sublime effect of the ancient roodscreens, before their mutilation under Edward the Sixth. The images are all ancient and were procured from some of the suppressed continental abbeys; the crucifix itself is of the natural size, and carved with wonderful art and expression; the images of our blessed Lady and St. John are less in proportion, which is quite correct. Immediately under tracery panels in front of the loft, are a series of ancient sculptures; the centre of which represents the consecration of St. Chad, patron of the church, the other refers to the life and glories of St. John the Baptist. On the mullions between the open panels, on foliated corbels, are eight images of prophets. The rood is richly gilt and painted, and it is proposed to continue the same decoration over the screen itself. At St. Alban's, Macclesfield, is a perpendicular screen, also surmounted by an ancient rood with images and lights. St. Mary's, Dudley, St. Oswald's, near Liverpool, St. Wilfred's, Manchester, are all furnished with roods and screens, revived faithfully from ancient authorities, enriched with paintings and gilding, ascended by a turret staircase, and in all respects similar to those which existed in the old English Churches previous to their desecration under Protestant ascendency. St. George's-

---

* Nicholl's Londinum Redivivum, vol. i. p. 21.

in-the-Fields, London, and St. Barnabas, Nottingham, both now erecting, will have spacious roodlofts ascended by double staircases; and at St. Giles's, Cheadle, a screen is in preparation with a ribbed and overhanging canopy, supporting a loft with a splendid rood; the whole of this screen will be enriched with gold and lively colours, and on the lower panels images of apostles and martyrs, painted in the severe style of Christian art. On referring to the engravings accompanying this article, it will be seen that a correct screen and roodloft, with its rood and images, has been erected in every church there figured, and that the English Catholics have revived this mystical and impressive feature of the ancient churches in all its integrity. The sacrilegious destruction of the roods under Edward the Sixth, their subsequent restoration in the reign of Queen Mary, and final demolition on the establishment of Protestant principles by Elizabeth, will be set forth at large hereafter.

Of embroidery and needlework, the writer most justly remarks:

" We may be allowed to ask, would not the time and ingenuity spent on worsted-work, satin-stitch, bead-work, and the like frivolities, be better employed if it were occupied in preparing an offering to God, for the adornment of His holy dwelling places ? Hour after hour is cheerfully sacrificed in the preparation of useless trifles for those charity bazaars, which would fain teach us that we *can* serve God and mammon : no time is then thought too much, no labour spared. But when an altar-cloth or carpet is to be provided, then the commonest materials and commonest work are thought good enough. Better examples were set in former times : as here and there a tattered piece of church embroidery still remains to tell us."

It is most gratifying to perceive that true ideas on these matters are fast spreading themselves,* and it is fervently to be hoped that they will eventually cause a better style of work to be introduced amongst those ladies who profess to embroider for the Church: at present, the generality of their productions, covered as they are with hearts, rosebuds, and doves, stand forth in all their *prettiness*, like valentine letters on a large scale; and truly it would seem as if they derived

---

* We most earnestly recommend the perusal of a work by the Rev. E. Paget, entitled "St. Antholin's or Old Churches and New," which is an admirable production, and enlarges considerably on some of the topics alluded to in the above extract.

all their ideas and authorities from such sources. It must, however, be observed in justice, that although the majority as yet most obdurately refuse to adopt true ideas when offered to them, still there are many glorious exceptions, of which the hangings in St. Chad's are ample testimony; and fresh converts are being continually made, even among those who seemed hopelessly entangled in modern trumpery.

From the few examples of ancient vestments that have escaped destruction, the generality of persons are but little acquainted with the extreme beauty of the embroidery worked for ecclesiastical purposes during the Middle Ages. The countenances of the images were executed with perfect expression, like miniatures in illuminated manuscripts.* Every parochial church, previous to the change of religion, was furnished with complete sets of frontals and hangings for the altars. What then must have been the overpowering splendour and glory of the cathedral and abbatial churches when decorated for the great festivals; the canopies, the needlework hangings, the monumental palls covered with heraldic devices, the altar-cloths, and, above all, the suits of sacred vestments,† when our bishops celebrated with the whole choir

---

* In the collection of ecclesiastical antiquities preserved at St. Mary's College, Oscott, are several specimens of copes and vestments of the fifteenth century, the orphreys of which are wonderful examples of ancient skill, the minutest details being perfectly expressed with the richest colouring.

† We read in the inventory of Lincoln, "twenty fair copes of the same suit, with three wheels of silver in the hoods.

" Item, five red copes of red velvet, with Katharine wheels of gold and orphreys, with images in tabernacles.

" Item, a cope of the root of Jesse.

" Item, thirteen copes of the same suit of blue velvet.

" Item, six copes of one suit broidered with angels, having this scripture, Da Gloriam Deo, with orphreys of needlework, of which four have the four evangelists in the morses, and the fifth a lamb in the morse.

" Item, eighteen copes of red satin of one suit, with orphreys of gold, and images."

There were upwards of two hundred and fifty copes, all of most costly material and elaborate embroidery, belonging to the cathedral church of Lincoln, till the latter part of Henry the Eighth's reign.

There were one hundred and twenty-eight copes, many exceedingly costly, belonging to the choir service of the cathedral church of St. Paul, London, besides those which were used for the church of St. Faith's, and various chapels attached to the mother church.

In the inventory of the ornaments belonging to the church at Peterborough, one hundred and seventeen copes are mentioned.

" York Minster.—Item, twenty-one copes of white velvet, of one suit, with gold orphreys.

" Item, eighteen blue copes with orphreys of red cloth of gold."

In all, three hundred and two copes belonging to the revestry of York Minster.

These are only a few examples, to show how splendidly our churches were furnished with vestments previous to their plunder by that sacrilegious monster Henry the Eighth.

filled with clergy, in copes, chasubles, and dalmatics, all of most costly material and exquisite detail? In some churches there were twenty or thirty copes in one suit, with a succession of subjects from the life of our Lord in the hoods and orphreys to correspond.

One of the great beauties of the ancient embroidery was its appropriate design; each flower, each leaf, each device had a significant meaning with reference to the festival to which the frontal or vestment belonged. This principle is completely overlooked at present; any design, so long as it is considered to look pretty, is introduced indiscriminately for all seasons, and in all situations. There is no distinction between the pattern of a drawing-room paper and that of a cope, or any perceptible difference in the figure of the stuff sold for dresses and that used in vestments; hence the ecclesiastical costume of the present day looks showy but not rich, and certainly fails in imparting dignity to the ministers of religion. On the contrary, the effect of the ancient vestments, which were exclusively ecclesiastical in their design, and conveyed a symbolic meaning by every ornament about them,* must have been so imposing and edifying, as to fill the beholder with reverence. England was famous for the production of embroidered vestments, insomuch that they were eagerly sought for all over Christendom, and known by the name of English work;† even in the Saxon times we read of nine albs‡ being sent as a present to Rome from this country,

---

* In the third volume of "Gerbert de Veturi Liturgia Alemannica," three copes of about the tenth century are accurately figured. They are divided into compartments, each containing a subject from the Old or New Testament, the images being so disposed on the half-circle as to appear upright when the cope was worn, and there are certainly not less than one hundred figures on each cope. The Earl of Shrewsbury has at present in his possession a cope of the twelfth century, formerly belonging to the nuns of Sion, divided all over in quatrefoils, each containing a saint or angel, and on the upper part the crucifixion of our Lord, all most exquisitely worked in silk.

A great number of crosses for chasubles, in needlework of the fifteenth century, are yet preserved in Catholic families; in the centre of these is usually the crucifixion of our Lord, while angels in the arms of the cross are raising the sacred blood in chalices; the mere inspection of these must convince every unprejudiced mind of the vast superiority and fitness of the sacred subjects selected for the orphreys of vestments in ancient days, over the mere scroll patterns and unmeaning ornaments that have been substituted in these latter times.

+ Such was the extreme beauty of the English vestments in the reign of Henry the Third, that Innocent the Fourth forwarded bulls to many English bishops, enjoining them to send a certain quantity of embroidered vestments to Rome, for the use of the clergy there.

‡ It must not be supposed that these embroidered albs were composed of lace flounces, in the ball dress style. Such monstrosities were not imagined for eight centuries after the period referred to. The embroidery of these albs

F

and offerings of the same kind were constantly being forwarded to the holy see, till the English schism. These facts are sufficient to show the high state of perfection to which the art of embroidery had arrived in this country during the *dark ages,* and are a complete refutation to those who are so desirous of proving that we were compelled to seek foreign aid in the production of our more costly and finished works. England, while Catholic, was a flower-garden of art; her Church was glorious indeed, and there was more real skill and Christian design exhibited in the erection of any one of her Cathedrals, than is now to be found in the united academies of Europe under the blasting influence of Protestantism and Paganism combined. Not only were all these splendid monuments of her ancient skill mutilated or destroyed, but the spirit which produced them was for a time entirely hid, we

---

consisted of sacred images wrought in the apparels; these apparels were compartments, of about two feet in length and one in width; they were attached to the alb nearly as low as the feet, before and behind, while lesser compartments of the same design and material were affixed to the lower extremity of the sleeve, above the wrist; the mystical signification of these apparels most probably referred to the wounds of our Lord; their use was universal in Christendom, and the ornaments on them were both costly and exceedingly beautiful. Albs with their apparels, are frequently mentioned in inventories of church vestments; they are to be perfectly distinguished on the effigy of every priest or bishop where any vestige of the original painting remains; and they are exceedingly conspicuous on all engraved monumental brasses of ecclesiastics, and in images painted on glass. In 1605, the tomb of Pope Boniface the Eighth, who died in 1305, was opened; the body was found entire, in full vestments, pontifically attired. The two apparels of the albs were filled with scripture histories, in gold and silk; on the front apparel, the history of our Lord, from the annunciation to the finding in the temple; on the back, the passion, resurrection, &c. Each apparel was three and-a-half palms long and a palm wide. A minute description of the vestments is given in John Rubens (Ross), an English Benedictine, in his " Bonifacius VIII ;" Rome, 1651 ; p. 346. On all the effigies of ecclesiastical persons prior to the sixteenth century, which are remaining in the churches at Rome, the apparels of the albs are most perfectly delineated : in the celebrated picture of the conversion of St. Jerome, the deacon, who is kneeling on the foreground, is habited in an apparelled alb ; and in Raphael's " Transfiguration," on the alb of a deacon who is kneeling in the upper corner of the picture, on the left hand, the apparels are shown on the sleeves. De Moleon, in his " Voyage Liturgique," calls these albs "albæ paratæ ;" and mentions several churches where they were used in France, when he wrote, as at St. Agnan d'Orleans, St. Maurice d'Angers, &c. His words are as follows : " L'aube a des paremens en bas conformes aux ornemens : ce qui s'appelle dans les brefs, Alba parata : on *s'en sert encore aujourdhui dans les églises cathédrales, et dans les anciennes abbayes.*" As De Moleon wrote only in the last century, the lace flounces must be of very recent introduction in France. Apparels precisely similar in pattern to those engraved on the monumental brasses of ancient churchmen, have been lately wove in gold and coloured silks, and are worn with the albs on festivals ; their cost is less than one-half of a modern bordering, and in them are revived, at one time, a striking emblem of our Lord's passion and the universal practice of the Church in the days of her glory.

will not say extinguished,—for now the spirit of the thirteenth century seems to animate many of her children in the nineteenth, and what may we not reasonably hope to see restored? The manufacture of precious stuffs has been lately revived,* and why should not many of the looms which have so long laboured to supply the changing demand of worldly fashion, be again employed in clothing the spouse of Christ—the Church—in her ancient glorious garb?

But we must most earnestly impress on the minds of all those who work in any way for the decoration of the altar, that the only hope of reviving the perfect style is by *strictly adhering to ancient authorities;* illuminated MSS., stained glass, and *especially brasses* (which can easily be copied by rubbing), will furnish excellent examples, and many of them easy of imitation.   We cannot yet hope to revive the expression and finish of the old work, but we may readily restore its general character, for many instances could be cited where this has been already most successfully accomplished in buildings engraved in this work; and with a little practice, it is easier and much sooner produced than the trifling no-meaning patterns of the modern style.   Is it not reasonable to suppose, that when the whole country was Catholic, and when the decoration of the Church formed the grand object on which the most ingenious efforts were bestowed, that the subject was far better understood than at present?   We may have made great improvements in steam-engines, but certainly not in frontals and orphreys; and York and Canterbury will furnish far better patterns than either Paris or Protestant Berlin.   The following works might be consulted with great advantage: *Shaw's Illuminated Ornaments; Shaw's Decorations of the Middle Ages; Waller's Brasses;* and to facilitate the object as much as possible, it is proposed to publish very shortly a series of ornaments, full size, as working-patterns.   It is proper to observe, that the heraldic law, of colour being always laid on metal, or metal on colour, should be strictly observed in embroidering; and one of the five canonical colours should be selected as a field for the whole work.   Velvet is the best material that can be used, after cloth of gold, for the ground.

The writer is not altogether correct in the observations he makes respecting stained glass.   The colours are now most perfectly restored to all their original brilliancy;† the soul

* The cloth of gold for the best suit of vestments offered to St. Chad's Church by the Earl of Shrewsbury, was manufactured at Spitalfields, London, and at a less cost than it could have been imported from Lyons.

† Another great point which has been lately attained is the thickness of the

and feeling of the old glass-painters is alone wanting; and even in this department, some surprising advances have recently been made; though closely following the style, touch, and manner of ancient artists, who were, for the most part, men of extraordinary talent; they expressed so much with simple means, almost all their effect is produced by mere lines or scraping out. The great mistake of modern glass-painters has been, in treating the panes of windows like pictures or transparencies with forcing lights and shadows. The old artists worked in a conventional manner, not through ignorance, but from science: they worked, in fact, *to suit their material.* The beautiful outline of the stone tracery is the better defined, by their manner of filling up the vacant spaces. They did not aim at a picture cut up with mullions, but they enriched the openings left by those mullions; and this principle was rigidly adhered to, till the decline of the pointed style. Those who climb up by means of ladders, and examine these windows in detail, can alone appreciate the wonderful merits of the execution: the grace displayed in the ramifications of foliage, and the tendrils of plants (especially in those windows executed immediately preceding and during the decorated period), is most admirable. Again, nothing can be conceived more elegant than the outline of the crockets, *merely perhaps scraped out.** And as for expression, the countenances are, in many cases, perfectly heavenly; full of devotion, and yet produced by mere lines. How do modern virtuosos and collectors boast in the possession of bacchanalian groups, painted by some *celebrated* pagan artist of the latter times! and what immense sums are paid for a Cupid or Venus, which are trumpeted forth as national acquisitions, while the most exquisite specimens of English art are utterly neglected, scarcely held from ruin by the mouldering bands to which they cling !† We shall probably incur the accusation of wild enthusiasm for the assertion we are about to make;

old glass: thin glass will never produce either the richness or the solemn tint of the ancient windows.

* Most of the minute work in the old glass is produced by scraping out; it is a very simple method, but requires the greatest skill in the artist.

† The parochial Churches of York contain many finer executed windows than the cathedral itself, and yet these are utterly neglected. Within the memory of persons yet living, whole windows have been suffered to fall out, and to be replaced *with white panes;* and at the present time some of the most interesting windows, especially at All Saints, North Street, and St. John's and St. Martin's, Micklegate, if *not speedily and effectually repaired will be irrecoverably ruined.* This, although distant from the scene of action, is yet a case for the "Camden;" for the windows alluded to are marvellously fine, and their loss would be irretrievable.

but we will say, that there are yet remaining in obscure churches—almost miraculously preserved from Protestant violence—specimens of native art, executed in the thirteenth century, which for sublimity of expression, simplicity of outline, dignity of position, and devotional effect, very far surpass anything yet introduced in the National Gallery of Painting; and the day will come, sooner or later, that tardy justice will be done to the wonderful talents of Catholic Englishmen in the days of faith; and the brutal stupidity of these who, utterly blinded to the merits of their native country, have filled every museum and institute with pagan casts, will be generally perceived and heartily execrated.[*]

The following remarks on bells are conceived in a most Catholic spirit:

" 55. It may not be out of place to say a few words on the subject of bells. You surely would not wish that instruments, consecrated like these to the praise of God, should be profaned by the foolish, profane, or self-laudatory inscriptions so often found on them. They, as all other parts of church furniture, are holy. The following are examples of ancient inscriptions on bells :

> Defunctos ploro, vivos voco, fulgura frango.
>
> Nos jungat thronis vere thronus Salomonis.
>
> AGNUS Sancte DEI, duc ad loca me requiei.
>
> Nomen Sancte JESU, me serva mortis ab esu.
>
> Sanguis Xpi, salva me ! Passio Xpi, conforta me !

Te laudamus, et rogamus	First bell,
Nomen JESU CHRISTI	Second bell.
Ut attendas et defendas	Third bell,
Nos a morte tristi.	Fourth bell.

To these, we add the inscription on the only bell of the Cathedral of Rouen that escaped the melting-pot at the great Revolution:

> "Laudo Deum verum, Plebem voco, congrego clerum,
> Defunctos ploro, Pestem fugo, Festa decoro."

The conclusion of this excellent tract is as follows:

" 58. Thus then imperfectly, but not, I hope, quite uselessly, have we completed our survey of a church and its ornaments. If

---

[*] What extraordinary infatuation is exhibited by those who dwell in cathedral towns, in the immediate vicinity of some glorious Church, capable in itself of furnishing ample instruction to every student that might present himself within its walls, when they pretend to found some school of art, and must needs import a shattered bull's head, and a volute as the beau-ideal of sculpture, whereby to pervert the minds and understandings of all the unfortuate youths who attend their institution.

everything else is forgotten, and two points only remembered, THE ABSOLUTE NECESSITY OF A DISTINCT AND SPACIOUS CHANCEL, and THE ABSOLUTE INADMISSIBILITY OF PEWS AND GALLERIES, in any shape whatever, I shall be more than rewarded. I have been writing in the name of a society; physically it may be weak in numbers and pecuniary resources, but morally strong in the zeal of its members and the goodness of its cause. It may, indeed, be years before the great truth is learnt, which that society hopes to be one of the instruments of teaching—the intrinsic holiness of a church, and the duty of building temples to God in some sort worthy of His presence. But learnt sooner or later it will be ; and to be allowed in any way to help forward so good a work, is a high privilege."

We can only observe, that the writer has accomplished his task in a manner quite worthy of the principles he here expresses, with the exception of some painful expressions; but where we find so much that is admirable and praiseworthy, we would fain, in charity, attribute them rather to the inconsistency of his present position, than to any graver cause.

As from the sublime to the ridiculous there is only one step, we may at once descend from the publications of the Camdenians, with their porches, fonts, aisles, screens and chancels, to notice a small book that has recently appeared, of the very opposite character, and entitled, *An Essay on Architectural Practice.* Although the title itself, implying the practice of architecture at the present time, would naturally lead us to expect something exceedingly bad, still the contents of the work exhibit church-building as fallen to a lower state of degradation than could possibly have been anticipated. The history of this production is briefly as follows: the architect having obtained the job of erecting one of the church commissioners' conventicles at the eastern end of the metropolis, instead of being content to pocket his commission and the disgrace of the production quietly, was resolved to set forth this genuine specimen of a London preaching-house of the nineteenth century, in the form of a distinct publication, under the above-mentioned title : having thus dragged forth this unsightly building from its local obscurity, and that at a time when a fine spirit is arising for real ecclesiastical architecture, he must not complain if he get as unmercifully treated as the enormity of his case deserves. Most architects, indeed, are content to build bad things; but to engrave, describe, and publish them afterwards, is something new, even in these pretending days. The illustrations consist of every possible dissection of the building, horizontal, vertical, lateral, transverse longitudinal—east, west, north, south—above, below, and all around; so that the edifice is perfectly set forth in all its poverty and ugliness. We have plans of concrete,—plans of footings,—plans of walls,—plans of pews,—plans of windows,—plans under galleries,—plans over galleries,—plans of slates,—plans of chimneys,—plans of gutters. As the funds allowed by church commissioners are too scanty to admit of much detail, there is not much set forth under this head; but the architect has atoned for the absence of bosses, capitals, niches, and tracery, by representing bricks, most ingeniously disposed in the form of barrel-drains, of varied diameters, and sections, of sewers and stink traps, with all the complicated principles of conveying dirty water from the gutter down a pipe, through a barrel-drain, into the common-sewer, thence to old Father Thames, and so on till lost in the expanse of ocean. In following the architect into these minutiæ, we have been hurried away by the muddy stream from the arrangement and appearance of the structure itself. The interior is a large room, covered with a low-pitched tie-beam roof; and if cleared out, would answer well for a *manège* or riding-school. The whole space is completely filled with pews, seats, and, of course, galleries, which are approached by staircases* at the west, and

---

* While thus noticing gallery staircases in churches, it may not be amiss to draw public attention to the atrocities that have lately been perpetrated in the venerable church of St. Saviour's, Southwark. But a few years since it was one of the most perfect second-class cruciform churches in England, and an edifice full of the most interesting associations connected with the ancient history of this metropolis. The roof was first stripped of its massive and solemn nave; in this state it was left a considerable time exposed to all the injuries of wet and weather; at length it was condemned to be pulled down, and in place of one of the finest specimens of ecclesiastical architecture left in London—with massive walls and pillars, deeply moulded arches, a most interesting south porch, and a splendid western doorway—we have as vile a preaching-place (with crowded galleries, gas-lights, &c.) as ever disgraced the nineteenth century. It is bad enough to see such an erection spring up at all; but when a venerable building is demolished to make room for it, the case is quite intolerable. Will it be believed, that under the centre tower in the transept of this once most beauteous church, *staircases on stilts* have been set up, exactly resembling those by which the company ascend to a booth on a race-course? We entreat every admirer of ancient architecture, every one who cherishes the least love for the ancient glory of his country's church, to visit this desecrated and mutilated fabric, and weep over its wretched condition, and then join in loud and lasting execrations against all concerned in this sacrilegious and barbarous destruction—ecclesiastical, parochial, or civil authorities, architect, builder, and every one in the least implicated in this business. Nothing but Protestantism and the preaching-house system could have brought such utter desolation on a stately church; in fact the abomination is so great that it must be seen to be credited.

carried up in two clumsy erections, intended to look like towers, but of an elevation and scale which at once betray their real purpose. *The style* of the building is what, in the classification of competition drawings, would be termed *Norman*—that is to say, the arches are not pointed; but in other respects, it bears no greater resemblance to the architecture of the tenth century, than it has in common with ordinary cellars, the Greenwich railway, or any round arched buildings. The illustrations are not, however, the most absurd portion of the publication; for the gravity and solemnity with which the most ordinary operations of building are described, are truly ridiculous: we have a full description of the different spots where holes were dug to ascertain the nature of the soil, of which remarkable excavations an accurate plan is inserted in the text. As the spade-handle was not, however, long enough to reach a sound bottom, the ingenious and novel experiment of boring was tried with complete success; by which it was ascertained, that for several feet the site was composed of accumulated rubbish (typical, perhaps, of the intended structure); this leads to a dissertation on concrete; then we have an account of the carting and stacking of bricks, mixing mortar, building the walls, and the whole method of erecting a church on the cheap and nasty principle, winding up, like the address of an actor on a benefit night, with thanks to every body, for their unparalleled efforts and exertions. We are, however, obliged to the author for this publication, for it must do good by its very absurdity; and combining as it does, at one view, so many abominations which are common to the modern practice of church building, it must convince every unprejudiced person of the absolute necessity of strictly adhering to ancient models and authorities in these matters, if we would erect churches at all worthy of their sacred purpose.

We now turn the work in question over to the tender mercies of the Camden Society, where it will not find more favourable treatment than it has met with from us, if we may judge by the tone of the following most admirable critique, which appeared in the first number of the *Ecclesiologist*, a monthly publication that has long been a desideratum, devoted exclusively to ecclesiastical researches and intelligence.

" A church has recently been erected in a very populous part of Cambridge, called New Town, and is now nearly completed, the whole of the exterior being finished, and the internal arrangements in a state of rapid progress. The church is intended to hold an indefinite number of people, that is, as many as can be packed in a small area by means of most extensive galleries, which are ingeniously contrived so as to run round and fill up every part of the interior ; insomuch that upon entering the church, it appears, at first sight, to be *all gallery*, and nothing else.

"The church is of no particular style or shape ; but it may be described as a conspicuous red brick building, of something between Elizabethan and debased perpendicular architecture. A low tower is added at the west end, in order that the rather doubtful ecclesiastical character of the edifice may not be mistaken, and for the purpose of containing, or rather displaying to advantage, three immense clock faces, which will doubtless be useful as well as ornamental appurtenances to the building. The general design of this edifice is marked by the fearless introduction of several remarkable varieties and peculiarities of arrangement, which are strictly original conceptions.

"The tower is low, and of rather plain design than otherwise; superfluity of ornament having been carefully avoided, lest it should be out of character with the rest of the building. The chief features of the tower are four heavy brick walls, having large four-centred belfry windows in the upper part, without cusping or mouldings, but filled up to the top with louvre slates. There are also four octagonal turrets, which rise a few feet above the battlements, and look very humble and unaspiring, as becomes a modest cheap church in these days of refined architectural taste. The most remarkable, and one which is likely soon to prove the most striking peculiarity of this tower, is a vast circular aperture in each of the three sides, for the reception of the clock or clocks already alluded to. These apertures, or rather chasms, are circular holes cut in huge square stones, the four spandrils or corners of which are beautifully ornamented with the figures 1, 1, 4 and 8, which give scope to ingenious combinations, and which may be read in such an order as to make the date of the year, 1841. The hole is large enough for a full-grown bullock to leap through, were he desirous to try the experiment, as the tumbler does through a hoop ; and we should say the sooner each of them is stopped up by a good large clock (that of St. Paul's Cathedral, if procurable second-hand, would answer pretty well,) the better, since the upper part of the tower has at present the novel and rather unpleasant appearance from a distance of standing upon four legs.

" The church is constructed of very red brick indeed, agreeably relieved at the corners by nice little white quoins of dressed ashlar, imparting a very picturesque appearance to the whole edifice. There are patterns, too, representing visionary trellis-work, playfully displayed in the construction in black bricks, which really have a delightful effect, though we fear that this is a plagiarism from the beautiful new brick church recently erected in Barnwell. It is intended, we presume, for a pied variety of Great St. Mary's in this town ; though others suppose it rather to be a travesty of the chapel of Magdalene College, Oxford.

"The windows of the aisles (for there are two real aisles, and a well developed clerestory lighted by rows of neat square cottage windows) are perhaps just a thought too large ; but if the mullions had not stood *quite* on the same plane with the wall, and the heads had been pointed instead of square, and the jambs had had something of a moulding, and the lights been cinquefoiled in the head and under the transom, they would not have looked altogether unlike church windows. But here we cannot sufficiently admire the ingenuity which has completely obviated any objection to their size by intercepting the upper half with galleries, which appear indeed to be supported on the transoms, though this is only an ingenious deception, since the mullions would most infallibly give way under the weight of such extensive structures when filled with people. There are real arches and piers inside ; none of your cheap cast-iron pillars, but sturdy brick columns, without capitals, covered over with plaster that looks at a reasonable distance very like stone, and supporting four-centered arches with neat discontinuous mouldings cast in the plaister. The roof is a kind of flat deal ceiling, with thin pieces of wood here and there to look like purlins, principals, &c. &c. ; and the whole, being varnished very brightly, looks as gay as the roof of the saloon in a first-rate steam ship. As the altar is not yet put up, and probably not yet thought of, we cannot say where it will be placed ; but we have been unable, upon the closest inspection, to discover any place adapted for its reception : indeed, we are inclined to fear that it has been forgotten altogether. The elevation of the east end is rather peculiar. There is *no chancel whatever ;* not even the smallest recess as an apology for one. But there is a beautiful vestry ; a low square building, lighted with square windows, and having an embattled parapet reaching as high as the sill of the east window. The interior is fitted up very snugly with a fire-place and other conveniences, and is indeed by far the most respectable part of the whole building. The gable of the nave is ornamented with a graduated parapet, which looks like a flight of perilous steps to a small cross which surmounts the highest point. As the architect perhaps intended to be symbolical herein, we shall say nothing of its appearance, nor of the great sprawling east window, if we may be allowed such a harsh expression, with consumptive-looking mullions and transom, and destitute of tracery. Both this and the west window in the tower are rather unsuccessful specimens of modern Gothic ; or perhaps we should have said, very good examples of modern, but very bad ones of ancient Gothic.

"We have thus briefly detailed the general features of this extremely interesting building, because we feel certain that those who have not seen it, cannot form a thoroughly correct and comprehensive idea of a CHEAP CHURCH OF THE NINETEENTH CENTURY."

We have seen and examined the building which has called forth these severe remarks, and we most willingly bear full testimony to their justice : indeed it is scarcely possible to speak in adequate terms of this wretched edifice ; erected as if in mockery, under the very shadow of so many beautiful specimens of ancient skill, which still remain in this venerable university. It is only by depicting modern deformities in forcible language that we can hope for their being remedied. Milk-and-water men never effect anything; they deserve drowning in their own insipid compositions.

We have been induced to give this extract at full length, first on account of its being the very best description of a Protestant church that has yet appeared; and secondly, as we perceived with much regret that owing to the sensitive feelings of some black sheep in the society, who protested against it on very absurd grounds, the committee, after some sensible observations in defence of the remarks, have consented, for the sake of peace, to withdraw them, and reprint the number in which they were contained. Now if the feelings of individuals are to be consulted instead of truth, no correct observations will ever be published; for in the present state of ecclesiastical architecture, if you allude to imitation stone, meagre tracery, gallery fronts, and the like, the observations can be so generally applied, that, as the poet says,

> " If you mention vice or bribe, you so point to all the tribe,
> Each one cries that was levelled at me,"

and the incumbents of five hundred new churches will take fire at once. We do hope, therefore, that in future the society will not compromise truth in any shape ; and they can well afford to spare those who are not prepared to take a high ground in these matters, for such individuals are mere drags on the grand revival. At all events the admirable remarks which drew forth this protestation will not be consigned to oblivion; they are here reproduced in full, and we hope they will be printed on a fly-sheet and circulated at architectural societies, competition committees, and church-building meetings, as Methodist sabbath-breaking denunciations are distributed in tea-gardens and steam-boats; they should be headed " *Beware of the Camden*," and hung up *in terrorem* in every church-competing architect's office, to deter those gentlemen from proceeding in the present wretched system, and lead them, if possible, into the old track.

We procced to notice several ecclesiastical structures, either lately erected or now in progress, which will show that some of the English Catholics, fully inheriting the zeal and feelings of their forefathers, are reviving Christian architecture in all its original spirit; and it is indeed gratifying to perceive, that those who work on the ancient foundation of faith, although slender in means and few in number, are enabled, by the blessing of God, to achieve far greater practical results than those of their countrymen who, possessing equal ardour in the good cause and vast temporal resources, are precluded by their present unfortuuate position from carrying out in practice their excellent intentions.

THE HOSPITAL OF ST. JOHN. PLATE V.

This hospital, of which the annexed plate represents a bird's-eye view, is now erecting in the village of Alton, Staffordshire, within half a mile of the seat of the Earl of Shrewsbury, by whose pious munificence it is being raised; and when completed it is intended for the following foundation: a warden and confrater, both in priest's orders; six chaplains or decayed priests, a sacrist, twelve poor brethren, a schoolmaster, and an unlimited number of poor scholars. To accommodate these various persons, the building will consist of a chapel, school, lodging for the warden, common hall, kitchen, chambers and library for the six chaplains, lodgings for the poor brethren, and a residence for the schoolmaster, all connected by a cloister. Of these buildings the chapel, school, warden's lodgings, part of the cloister; and schoolmaster's house are already completed, and a few years will suffice to finish the remaining portions of the edifice as shown in the view. The whole is constructed of hewn stone in the most solid and durable manner, and the principal roofs, as well as flooring joists, and beams, are worked in English oak. Immediately facing the western end of the school is a stone cross raised on steps; the base is quadrangular, with an Evangelist within a quatrefoil on each face; the upper part of the shaft terminates in a foliated cap supporting a quadrangular niche containing an angel bearing emblems of our Lord's passion on every side; at the summit of which is a floreated cross of stone. Over the porch, or entrance to the cloister and warden's lodgings, is a niche containing an image of St. John the Baptist with the lamb; and another image of St. Nicholas with the three boys is placed in a canopied niche in the west window of the school. The side windows of this

Saint ⚜ Iohne ⚜ ho

∴ S̶ JOHNS CHAPEL. ALTON ∴ ꙮꙮ

N⁰ 6

school are filled with painted glass, consisting of armorial bearings, figured quarries and borders; and round the lower lights of the seven windows is the following inscription: "Of your charity pray for the good estate of John the sixteenth Earl of Shrewsbury, who founded this hospital in honour of St. John the Baptist, Anno Domini 1840. St. John pray for us. Amen."

To the eastward of the school is the chapel, an interior view of which is here given, Plate VI. This portion of the building has been most carefully finished, and contains much decoration. The whole floor is laid with figured tiles, charged with the Talbot arms and other devices. The benches are precisely similar to those remaining in some ancient parish churches in Norfolk, with low backs filled with perforated tracery of various patterns; the poppy-heads are all carved, representing oak and vine leaves, lilies, roses, lions, angels, and other emblems. The chancel is divided off by a rich screen, surmounted with a rood and images. The shields in the brestsummer are all charged with sacred emblems in gold and colours. The rood is also richly gilt. Each principal of the roof springs from an angel corbel, bearing each a shield or a scripture; the braces, tiebeams, rafters, and purloins of this roof are moulded, and the spandrils filled with open tracery. On each side of the east window is a niche with images of St. Katharine and St. Barbara. The reredos and altar are both worked in alabaster;* the former consists of a series of richly canopied niches surmounted by an open brattishing; images of the apostles holding the emblems of their martyrdom, with our blessed Lord in the centre, occupy these niches. The altar itself consists of three large and three lesser compartments, with the images of our blessed Lady, St. John the Baptist, and St. Alban, with two angels seated on thrones

---

* It is to be hoped that the use of this beautiful material, which was constantly used by the Catholic artists in their more elaborate works, will be generally revived. It is admirably adapted for the finest style of carving, easily worked, exceedingly durable, and capable of receiving a high polish. The best quarries are at Tutbury, in Staffordshire; but at present they remain quite neglected, being only casually worked, when materials for plaister are required. Blocks of a sufficient size for sepulchral effigies might be easily procured, and at a moderate cost. Many of the most beautiful ancient monuments were worked in alabaster; also reredoses of altars, and generally images. In the churchwardens' accounts in the time of Edward VI. (when the spoliation and destruction of the English parochial churches was commenced), we frequently find entries of sums received for *alabaster work sold by weight as material for making plaster!!!* And at that fatal period many of the most exquisite productions in this material perished in the kiln.

bearing the lamb and cross. The sunk work is picked out in azure; the raised mouldings and carved ornaments gilt, and the remainder polished alabaster, similar to some of the costly tombs yet remaining in Westminster and other churches. On each side of this altar silk curtains are suspended on rods. The cross is an exquisite specimen of ancient silver work of the fifteenth century, made, as the inscription round the foot relates, by one Peter, for a German bishop, who bore the charge for the love of Christ crucified. This precious relic of Christian art is parcel-gilt, and covered with ornaments and images of wonderful execution. A pair of parcel-gilt silver candlesticks have been made to correspond in style with this cross; they are richly chased, engraven, and ornamented with enamels.

On the gospel side of the chancel is a small chapel, containing an altar for the reservation of the most holy sacrament, which is placed within a gilt tower surmounted by a cross. This chapel communicates with the chancel by a richly moulded and paneled doorway, and also by an arched opening of the same description, containing a high tomb with tracery and emblems, to serve for the sepulchre at Easter.

On the north side of the chapel is a three-light window, and in every light an angel bearing the cross, the pillar, and the holy name, with this scripture, "By thy cross and passion, O Lord, deliver us." In the east window are also three lights, with an image of our blessed Lady with our Lord in the centre, St. John the Baptist with the lamb on the right, and St. Nicholas, vested as he used to say mass, with the three children, on the left, all under rich canopies; and in the upper part of the window, angels with labels and scriptures. The side windows are filled with ornamental quarries and rich bordures and quatrefoils, containing the emblems of the four Evangelists, the annunciation of our blessed Lady, the pot of lilies with the angelical salutation entwined, and the holy name of our Lord.

The sacristy is fitted with oak almeries for vestments, and furnished with such sacred vessels and ornaments as are required in the solemn celebration of the divine office. The cloister is paved with figured tiles, and the windows contain many arms and emblems in stained glass; while the walls are enriched with niches containing sculptured representations of our Lord's passion, and other edifying mysteries of the Christian faith.

The site that has been selected for this hospital is one of

the most beautiful and suitable for such an edifice that can
well be imagined. From the north wing, which stands on the
verge of a steep rock some hundred feet in height, a most
extensive view of the rich valleys and surrounding country is
obtained; while to the south a well-sheltered slope is admirably calculated for gardens. From its immediate vicinity
to the ruins of the ancient castle,* with its overshadowed
moat and winding paths, it offers easy access to the most
retired and sheltered walks, well suited to the meditation of
its aged inmates; and being only a few paces distant from the
village, it will afford all the consolations of the regular divine
office, that will be celebrated daily within its walls to the
Catholic inhabitants. When viewed from the opposite hills,
its turrets and crosses seem to form but one group with the
more venerable tower of the parochial church and the varied
outline of the castle buildings. As no reasonable cost has
been spared by the noble founder in the erection of this
building, when completed it will present, both in its exterior
and internal arrangements, a perfect revival of a Catholic
hospital of the old time, of which so many were seized, demolished, and perverted by the sacrilegious tyrant Henry
and his successors in church plunder; and in lieu of these
most Christian and pious foundations for our poorer brethren,
prisons are now substituted for those convicted of poverty,—
a state voluntarily embraced by thousands in days of faith,
as one of great perfection and most pleasing to Almighty
God, but in these modern and enlightened times accounted a
heinous offence.

---

* Of this castle Buck the antiquary gives the following account : " It is a
castle more ancient than the Norman conquest. In the 22d of Henry II,
Bertram de Verdun was lord of it, whose residence it was, and that of the
family, till the 3d of Edward II. During the minority of Thomas de Verdun,
William Fitz Richard had the care of his estates; the manor had not less than
ten (some say fourteen) villages belonging to it. Male issue failing, it came by
marriage to the Furnivals, who held it in two successions; when by the same
means it came to Thomas Nevil, brother to the Earl of Westmoreland; but he
also leaving an only daughter, it passed by her to the famous Sir John Talbot
(with her other estates), who by right of his wife was lord of this castle, and
Lord Furnival, but afterwards created Earl of Shrewsbury, in which family it
still remains." The ruins of this castle, as engraved in Buck's work, appear to
have been very considerable in his time, but they have been sadly demolished
during the last century, huge masses being frequently hurled down for the
purpose of mending the roads. The ravages were stopped by the late earl; and
these interesting remains are now preserved with the greatest care. The exact
situation of the original gateway, with its circular towers, was ascertained by
excavation on clearing away the rubbish in 1840. At that time a most interesting thurible of the twelfth century was discovered buried in the moat, and close
to the site of the castle chapel.

THE CISTERCIAN MONASTERY OF ST. BERNARD, LEICESTERSHIRE.
PLATE VII.

It is now 744 years since the monastery of Citeaux was founded in a wild and desert place near Chalon-sur-Saone, by blessed Robert abbot of Molesme, and a few holy monks who were his companions, that they might the better serve God in austerities, silence, mortifications, and prayer, according to the primitive rule of St. Benedict of glorious memory.

From this edifying example devout men arose in all the countries of Christendom, eager to follow in the path they had so wisely chosen; and through the fervour and zeal of this new and rigid order, England soon beheld some of the noblest churches that ever graced this glorious land arising in the solitude of her forests and uncultivated valleys. Even yet, how famous are the names of Fountains, Furness, Tintern, Joreval, Kirkstall, and a host of others,* although the glory of their sanctuaries is departed, and little more than prostrate pillars and crumbling walls remain to attest their ancient dignity, so desolate indeed do they seem, and so passed away is the generation of men by whom they were raised and inhabited; so changed is the spirit of mortification, solitude, and prayer, which instigated their erection; that when we behold the chilling spectacle of their sad decay, we might indeed mourn the ancient faith as utterly departed. But so unsearchable are the decrees and ways of God, that monastic institutions have revived in this land by the means of a convulsion that would have seemed as the annihilation of their very existence.

Whilst Protestant tyranny and fanaticism ruled in this country with an iron rod, many of the scattered religious found refuge in foreign lands; and when the continent in its turn became the scene of revolution, anarchy, and infidelity, England gladly received and sheltered the communities that by unjust laws had been so long separated from her. Amongst others, the English Cistercians from the monastery of La Trappe† returned to their native soil; and to these the com-

---

* " The first English monastery of Cistercians was founded at Waverley, in Surrey, A. D. 1129 ; and in the reign of king Edward the First, there were sixty-two houses of this order in England."—Stevens' Continuation to Dugdale.

† It is erroneously imagined by many persons that the monks of La Trappe are a new order, whose rule is framed with unexampled and unnatural severity. But, in fact, they are only a reform of the Cistercians, established by the famous Abbé Rancy, in the monastery of La Trappe, in France, from whence the

munity of Mount St. Bernard owes its existence. It is not necessary to enter at length into the various vicissitudes they encountered, or the circumstances that led them eventually to establish a monastery in Leicestershire, as these will be detailed at length in a separate publication on the subject by Ambrose Lisle Phillipps, Esq, that will shortly appear; but it must be no small consolation to every Catholic mind, that in the nineteenth century, a community of men flourish in the very heart of England, bound by the same rules, practising the same austerities, devotions, and charity, wearing the same habit, and in all respects like to the devout men of old, whose works and lives are yet the theme of admiration and respect among men of true piety and antiquarian research.

The prospect of the monastery, which is taken from the south-west, represents the edifice as complete, and gives a general idea of the locality in which it is placed. The country immediately surrounding the monastery is exceedingly wild and romantic, more, indeed, resembling Sicilian than English scenery. Irregular masses of granite rocks of most picturesque outline surround the land cultivated by the monks; and as the situation is exceedingly elevated, the extensive prospects which open out beyond these from different points of view, are truly glorious to behold. The monastery is sheltered on the north side by a huge rock, on the summit of which it is purposed to erect a calvary, as shown in the view, which will be visible from an immense extent of the surrounding country. Although, from its exposed position, the land is far from desirable in an agricultural point of view, the unceasing toil of the religious has so far overcome natural difficulties, that a considerable portion of the ground is already brought into excellent cultivation. The whole of the regular buildings, cloister, chapter-house, refectory, dormitory, calefactory, guest-house, prior's lodgings, lavatory, kitchen offices, &c., are now actually finished; and arrangements are in progress for completing as soon as possible a

---

appellation of Trappists has been applied most improperly to those religious who returned to the strict observance of the primitive rule of the order, which although it may seem unsupportably austere in these days of decayed zeal and fervour, was only the ordinary state of religious life observed by the ancient monks. The extraordinary piety and fervour of the Abbé de Rancy naturally excited the animosity of those lax members of the religious orders, of which there were but too many instances in the corrupt age in which he commenced his reform ; and many infamous calumnies were published against him. The best refutation of these is to be found in a small work entitled " Défence de la Trappe," of which the celebrated Father Thiers was the supposed author.

sufficient portion of the church to enable the monks to celebrate the divine office with becoming solemnity; when this
is achieved, the community will leave their present temporary
edifice, and enter on the occupation of this new monastery.

The whole of the buildings are erected in the greatest
severity of the lancet style, with massive walls and buttresses, long and narrow windows, high gables and roofs,
with deeply arched doorways. Solemnity and simplicity are
the characteristics of the monastery, and every portion of the
architecture and fittings corresponds to the austerity of the
order for whom it has been raised. The space inclosed by
the cloisters is appointed for the cemetery; a stone cross,
similar to those which were formerly erected in every churchyard, will be set up in the centre, and the memorials of departed brethren will be inserted on plain wooden crosses at
the head of the graves. The view from this inclosure is
particularly striking. From the nature of the material used (a
sort of rubble granite) and the massiveness of the architecture,
the building already possesses the appearance of antiquity;
and this being combined with the stillness of the place and
the presence of the religious, clad in the venerable habits of
the order, the mind is most forcibly carried back to the days
of England's faith.

The second plate, VIII. represents the interior of the conventual church as designed, taken from the western end of the
nave. The arches are shewn as springing from pillars of
nine feet in circumference, ornamented with foliated caps.
The framing of the roof, which will be decorated with painting,
is open to the church, and springs from stone corbels, level
with the base of clerestory windows; the high altar is at the
eastern end, against a reredos of arched panels, below the
triple lights of the end gable; four massive pillars support
the arches of the centre tower, which is shewn in the external
prospect. On the eastern walls of the transepts are two
altars, that on the south dedicated in honour of our blessed
Ladye, and the northern one in honour of St. Joseph. As the
chapter-house joins close to the southern wall of the transept,
a rose window will be erected in the gable, and three large
lancet lights on the opposite end; the sacristy is on the
south side, and forms in the plan a continuation of the transept gable wall nearly as far eastward as the termination of
the church. The whole choir is surrounded by spacious aisles
for solemn processions. The stalls for the religious extend

✠ S BERNARD ABBEY CHVRCH ⚜⚜⚜⚜⚜

down a considerable portion of the nave,* as far as the large
stone rood loft, shewn in the engraving, which will be ascended by two stone staircases immediately behind the prior's
and subprior's stalls. This roodloft is supported by three open
arches, the two side ones containing.stone altars, surmounted
by paintings and other enrichments The custom of placing
altars in the rood screens, which is exceedingly ancient, originated in the monastic churches: we are not aware of existing instances where they occur in any other. The reason
is obvious: as the people were entirely excluded from the
eastern portion of the church, and confined to that part
of the nave which remained between the rood loft and the
western end, the monks naturally resorted to this expedient
for administering the consolation of the holy sacrifice to
such of the faithful as might visit their churches through
devotion. It may be further remarked, in support of this
reason, that these altars are found only in such of the
churches and cathedrals as were either originally monasteries, as Peterborough, Gloucester, St. Alban's; or were
served by monks, as Durham and Norwich. The rood screen
and altars of Durham have perished; but the annexed note† will

---

* Examples of these are yet to be found at Westminster, Gloucester, Winchester, Tewkesbury, St. Alban's, and Norwich.
+ " In the body of the church, between two of the highest pillars supporting
the west side of the lantern, opposite the choir door, was Jesus' altar, where
Jesus' mass was sung every Friday in the year, and on the back-side of the said
altar was a high stone wall, at each end whereof was a door, which was locked
every night, and called the two·rood doors, for the procession to go forth and
return at; betwixt the two doors was Jesus' altar, placed as aforesaid, and
each end of the altar was closed up with fine wainscot, like to a porch, adjoining
to each rood door, finely varnished with red varnish. In the wainscot, at the
south end of the altar, were four great almeries, to preserve the chalices and
silver cruets, and two or three suits of vestments, and other ornaments belonging to the said altar, for holy and principal days; and at the north end of the
altar, in the wainscot, was a door to come into the said porch, which was
always locked. There was also standing against the wall a most curious fine
table, with two leaves to open and shut; comprehending the passion of our
Lord Jesus Christ, richly set in fine lively colours, all like burnished gold, as
he was tormented on the cross; a most lamentable sight to behold; which
table was always locked but on principal days. Also the fore part of the said
porch, from the utmost corner of the porch to the other was a door, with two
broad leaves to open from side to side, all of fine thorough carved work; the
height was somewhat above a man's breast, and the upper part stricken full of
iron spikes, so that none should climb over; which door hung all on gimmers,
and had clasps on the inside to fasten them. And on principal days, when any
of the monks said mass at the said altar, then the table standing thereon was
opened, and the door with two leaves that composed the fore-part of the said
porch was set open also, that every man might come in and see the table in
the manner aforesaid.

G 2

enable the reader to understand their ancient position in that noble church. We believe that at Norwich Cathedral, since the *improvements* in the choirs, all traces of the altars which stood on either side of the choir door have disappeared; but a few years since the outline of the altars and the reredoses themselves were most distinctly marked. At St. Alban's the screen across the nave is called St. Cuthbert's: the altar, as at Durham, stood in the centre, with a doorway at each side, leading into the choir; and there is every reason to suppose a similar screen formerly existed at Romney Abbey. The arrangement of the rood screen, as shewn in the plate, is therefore quite correct for a monastic church; the depth of the arches under which the altars are placed, is considerable; and, with the staircases, this loft will occupy one bay of the nave in width; above the screen, the rood* will be fixed with the

---

"There was also in the height of the wall, from pillar to pillar, the whole story and passion of our Lord, wrought in stone, and curiously gilt; and also above the said story and passion, there was the whole story and picture of the twelve apostles, very artificially set forth, and finely gilt, extending from one pillar to the other; and on the top, above all the aforesaid stories, was set up a border artificially wrought in stone, with marvellous fine colours, and gilt with branches and flowers; insomuch that the more a man looked on it the more was his desire to behold it; and, though in stone, it could not have been finer in any kind of metal. And likewise on the top of all stood the most famous rood that was in all the land, with the picture of St. Mary on one side, of our Saviour and St. John on the other; with two glittering archangels, one on the one side of St. Mary and the other on the other side of St. John. So that for the beauty of the wall, stateliness of the picture, and the liveliness of the painting, it was thought to be one of the grandest monuments in the church."

Antiquities of Durham Abbey, pp. 35–6.

The altar, rood, and images, were all demolished and defaced in the reign of Edward the Sixth, and the screen itself was destroyed soon after.

* A very curious account is given in Peck's "Stamford," chap. iv. p. 3, illustrative of the antiquity of roods. It refers to the sacking and plunder of the monastery at Burg, A. D. 1069; and it appears that on the robbers effecting an entrance into the church, *they got up to the rood*, and took away a crown from our Lord's head, a crown made entirely of gold. From this description we not only gather the existence of a rood set up in a high place in the church, but also that the image on the same was one of those mystical representations of our Lord, as a king vested in royal robes, fastened to a rich cross, which were frequent in early times; and the miraculous crucifix still preserved in the second chapel on the gospel side of the nave in Amiens cathedral, is of this style. This conventional manner of treating the sublime and overpowering mystery of our Lord's sacrifice on the cross, is truly beautiful; and it will probably be revived ere long, with many other long-forgotten but profound and admirable conceptions of the Middle Ages. The cross itself was treated from the earliest times as an emblem of glory. Hence, whether it was carved on sepulchral slabs, erected on churches, set up on roods, embroidered on altar cloths or vestments, it was invariably more or less floreated with enriched terminations branching out, as the fruitful and never-fading source of the Christian's brightest hopes. Many of the crosses erected in England were, in themselves, most beautiful structures, and of the richest design. A large

Irvie Chapel near Pomfret &c.

No. 9

Church of the Sacred Heart of Jesus.

Church of the Sacred Heart of Jesus.

appropriate images, all richly painted and gilt. The upper extremity of the cross will be upwards of fifty feet in height from the level of the pavement, and the width across the arms about twelve feet. By the rules of the Cistercian order, the rood loft is used for all its ancient purposes, and will be provided with letterns, standards for lights, and other necessary furniture.

JESUS CHAPEL, NEAR POMFRET, PLATES IX AND X.

This edifice has been erected by Mrs. Tempest, who resides at the Grange, near Pomfret, to serve as a private chapel to the mansion with which it communicates, by means of a cloister on the north side. It consists of a nave, chancel, chantry, chapel containing a family vault, and a sacristry : the accompanying plate will afford a correct idea of its style and appearance. The architecture is that of the decorated period, and to the smallest details has been carefully and faithfully revived from original authorities. The niches on each side of the chancel window contain images of our Blessed Lady and the angel Gabriel, and the Holy Trinity in the centre niche of the gable. A belfry for the Sanctus is erected on the eastern end of the nave, and a floreated cross on the centre of the west gable. A massive and deeply moulded stone arch leads from the nave to the chancel, across which an oak screen of open panels, surmounted by a rood, has been erected. The roof of the nave is waggon-headed, divided by and divided into compartments by the principals of the roof, which are again subdivided by moulded ribs into panels, diapered in colours. The ceiling of the chancel is arched, also divided into compartments by ribs, but of a richer character than that of the nave; at each intersection is a boss, carved with emblems of the passion and

---

plain cross seems to be the extent to which the imagination of those who design these things at the present day on the continent will reach, and these are not unfrequently painted a bright green. In England the case is in some respects worse, for, the original intention of these holy emblems being disregarded, they have been prostituted to the vilest party purposes ; and the design of one of those truly beautiful and appropriate Eleanor crosses has been degraded to serve for the memorial of three of those miserable ecclesiastics who betrayed the church of which they were such unworthy members, and were mainly instrumental in the overthrow not only of the material crosses which had been raised by the piety of our forefathers, but that true and ancient faith which had shone so conspicuous in the English Church for so many succeeding generations, and which, down to that fatal period, which severed this country from the unity of Christ's Church, had covered the face of the land with the most glorious monuments that the skill and energy of man ever raised in honour of Almighty God.

other devices; and from each of these spring four foliage cusps, corresponding to the angles of the panels. The relieved portions of this ceiling are pricked out in gold and colour; the field is painted azure, powdered with stars and suns. All the windows are filled with stained glass; those of the nave contained figured quarries, rich borders, and quatrefoils filled with sacred emblems; in the east window of the chantry, the centre light is filled with an image of our Ladye with our Lord, under a canopy, and a serpent crushed beneath her feet: the two other lights contain the emblems of the four Evangelists, and the holy name in bordered quatrefoils. The upper part of the window is filled with angels, holding labels and scriptures.

The east window of the chancel contains the crucifixion of our Lord, the adoration of the wise men, and the resurrection, with appropriate scriptures. The side window of the chantry chapel is filled with armorial bearings of the Tempest family. On the Gospel side of the chancel is a richly ornamented niche, which is also open towards the chantry, and within it a high tomb to serve for the sepulchre at Easter. Immediately opposite to this are the sedilia, with crocketed canopies and pinnacles, and a sacrarium of the same ornamental character. The front of the principal altar is divided into five compartments or niches, with crocketed gablets, and each containing an image. The altar of the chantry is plain, and hung with a frontal of velvet, relieved with gold embroidery. Each altar is furnished with a pair of candlesticks and a crucifix on standing crosses. Curtains of silk are suspended on projecting rods on each side of the chancel altar, and on the upper steps are placed two high standards for the elevation candles. There is also a suspended lamp to burn before the blessed sacrament. The floors of the chancel and chantry chapel are laid with incrusted tiles of various patterns, similar to those with which the ancient churches were originally paved; and in all respects this chapel presents a very faithful revival of a small religious edifice of the fine period of Edward the Third.

BISHOP'S HOUSE, BIRMINGHAM. PLATE XI.

Next in importance to the erection of the church itself, is that of a suitable edifice for the habitation of those ecclesiastics who are appointed to serve its altars, and minister spiritual and temporal consolation to the faithful who flock within its walls. Hence we hail with no small gratification

N° II.   ✠ Bishops house Birmingham new view.

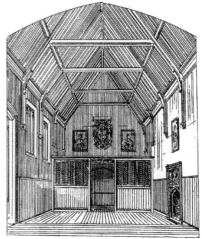

£ THE COMMON HALL

the erection of the present building, which is a consoling proof of the great revival of ancient principles in this most neglected branch of ecclesiastical architecture. We say *most neglected,* for even those who admitted the principle of imitating in some respects the ideas and style of our Catholic ancestors in their churches, rejected with ridicule all suggestions of following them in other matters; and, on the pleas of economy and convenience, have descended to the erection of the vilest sash-window and street-door residences that ever were raised.* Now, with respect to economy, it is impossible to build substantially in any style so cheap as the pointed or Christian; and, as to convenience, our ancestors were by no means such fools, or such comfortless barbarians as is generally imagined

---

* When this error has been avoided, the residences for the clergy have been made to look extremely like portions of the church ; and what at a short distance might appear as a transept, or a chancel, is discovered on a nearer approach to be nothing more than an ill-constructed house, whose several floors, by dint of blackened glass and other contrivances, are disguised into long-looking lancet windows ; while the clerestory serves the domestics for an attic, and the supposed crypt contains the cooking department, with even meaner offices ; and the building which had passed for a cruciform church, from a casual external survey, presents, on entering, a mere nave, which must naturally appear much smaller than it really is from the disappointment of the spectator.—We know of one case, where parlour, dining room, and bed chamber are all lighted from what appears externally to be the east window of the chancel, while the maid servant receives air from two huge quatrefoils in the tracery of the said window, the smoke from all these rooms being carried up a *flue turret* and perforated pinnacle. It is impossible to describe half the indecencies that must and do arise from men presuming to make their habitations under the roof of a building that should be solemnly consecrated to God alone ; and it is almost difficult to reconcile the existence of such an abuse with the extreme reverence and veneration with which all members of the Catholic Church are necessarily bound to regard all that is connected with the worship of Almighty God, and the sacred character which is imparted even to the material walls of a church. Besides, a church which forms part of a house will never be viewed or entered with the peculiar respect that it should command ; it sinks to the level of an ordinary place : servants cleanse the sanctuary as they do an entry; the thuribles and candlesticks are carried for convenience to the kitchen, vestments are kept in bedrooms. The exclusive character of all these things is soon lost, and irreverence succeeds. Then, instead of solemn-sounding bells, preparing the mind for prayer and sacrifice, we have rapping of knockers, closing of doors, shrill calls of domestics, and in some instances the savoury odours of kitchens overpowering the incense itself. Now all these things have originated in straightened necessity, but they should not continue through indifference; and very lately new buildings have been erected on a plan which must necessarily entail all these wretched consequences. How utterly dead must a man be, we will not say to mystical reasons alone, but to natural ones also, who builds a chimney-stack in place of the east window, turns an aisle into an entry, and lights his kitchen from the sanctuary ! Yet such and worse exist—nor shall we be readily delivered from them except by conflagration, which catastrophe is not by any means improbable, considering the ordinary risk which is attached to dwelling-houses.

by the moderns, who seem to derive all their ideas on these matters from delapidated buildings, unfurnished and uninhabited perhaps for centuries; a modern empty house looks miserable enough in all conscience after it has been vacated for only a few weeks; but only let us conceive its appearance after fifty years' neglect, which is the longest period which can be assigned for *its existence in any shape;* surely an old specimen of six times that age would then appear to no small advantage by its side. Under the name of modern convenience, people have been cheated into thin walls and plaster, in place of solid construction and oak beams. Of course there are sundry practical improvements made from time to time, which could and should be engrafted on old principles; but we have cast off in too many instances strength and real convenience, for empty display and cheap magnificence; and a modern house, with its cracking plaster and compo, peeling paper, rubbed off graining, marble veneers, dirty paint, and faded finery, is an erection that could not have arisen in any less fictitious age than the present.

But to return to our object. Ecclesiastical residences were always erected in harmony of design with the sacred structures to which they formed necessary appendages, that is to say, they *exhibited a solid, solemn, and scholastic character, that bespoke them at once to be the habitations of men who were removed far beyond the ordinary pursuits of life.* If we turn to the Vicar's Close at Wells, the hospital of St. Cross, or any of the collegiate or conventual buildings which remain, defaced and modernized as they are, they inspire reverence and respect; and what must have been their effect as originally left by their pious founders? This impression on the mind is not produced by richness of detail, for they are remarkably plain for the most part; but it is owing to the *absence of all artificial resources, and the severity and simplicity in which they have been raised;* there is no attempt at concealment, no trick, no deception, no false show, no mock materials; they appear as true and solid as the faith itself. Who does not feel some instinctive respect as he passes under the vaulting of an old gate-house and finds himself in a cloistered quadrangle? In such a place the mind is predisposed to reverence the ministers of religion; they seem as if occupying a position exclusively their own, and where they hold undisturbed right to teach and command; and as regards the ecclesiastics themselves, do not these arches, these mullioned windows, these cloistered alleys, tend to cherish and preserve within their breasts that gravity and religious composure so essential to the high state to which they belong. How violent is the contrast between the choir of a cathedral and the drawing-room of an Anglo-Protestant Prebendary, with its piano, nick-knacs, mirrors, and ottomans! surely the church was not intended to be the only place where the thoughts of God were to be imparted and cherished,—else why those long cloisters, that solemn chapter-room, that vast refectory, that common hall, those oratories, those crosses, those saintly images and emblems, those studious chambers and solemn buildings which our Catholic ancestors erected around every sacred pile? they knew that devotion *in* the sanctuary was only to be obtained by gravity and solemnity *without*. The ancient ecclesiastics did not perform parts in churches for a brief hour, and then put off the cleric with the surplice,* but carried their reverend garb and demeanour throughout every ordinary action in which they were engaged; and this it would not have been possible for them to have performed had they not resided in the solemn and retired structures provided for them. But if such edifices were found necessary for the promotion of regularity and discipline in the days of faith, and in times when the clergy had such vast resources in mutual support, how much more are they required amongst us at the present time, when our ecclesiastics are scattered in populous towns, frequently alone and unsupported, and where almost every spot, except their own domain, is poisoned with heresy, infidelity, and licentiousness! The only resource left in such a situation is to create an ecclesiastical atmosphere, a green spot in the desert, where both the architecture and fittings of the edifice breathe the reverend spirit of ancient days, and where the man of God, consecrated to the all-important work of leading his countrymen back to the true paths, with cassock and crucifix, may hold secret communion of soul with those glorious churchmen of old, whose fervent and mortified spirit he strives to imitate. Nor will such a residence, so different from the worldly habitations (filled with cheap and vulgar show) which surround it, fail in producing the most salutary effect on those souls who, filled with vague impressions of ancient Catholic solemnity, are seeking where they may find

---

* A striking instance of the great reverence with which the ancient churchmen regarded the celebration of the divine office, is to be found in the construction of several sacristies at Rouen cathedral, and other places, which are provided with a chamber where the hebdomadarius who sung the chapter-mass remained during the week, in silence and meditation.

a realization of the ideas they have imbibed in the study of past ages, and finding it not at the neat family parsonage, nor at the modernised canonry,* come .with trembling hopes to the once despised priests of the old faith.

Such are some of the ideas which suggested the absolute necessity of erecting a residence for the bishops and clergy of St. Chad's cathedral, corresponding in style and arrangements with the old ecclesiastical houses. The ground selected for this purpose is situated immediately opposite to the church, and being nearly ten feet lower on the north side, admits of increased accommodation in the base story of that wing; by

---

* The horrible mutilations of the ancient ecclesiastical residences attached to cathedrals, in order to render them at all suitable to the altered style of living, as practised by the present race of bishops, deans, canons, &c., afford the most striking examples of modern degeneracy; and are in themselves convincing proofs that the married worldly clergy of the day, are utterly unsuited for the venerable habitations which they occupy, and the glorious churches that they profess to serve. The great hall has been generally floored in the height, and subdivided into bed-chambers; while the chesnut roof, with its massive timbers and moulded braces, has become a mere dark attic, used as a depository for lumber, or for drying linen. It is almost superfluous to observe, that the domestic chapel has in every instance been degraded to some secular purpose, or totally destroyed. In one case it serves the canon's lady, or Mrs. Archdeacon, as a boudoir, where she deposits her nick-knacs and albums; in another it is used for a wash and brew-house, a huge copper occupying the place of ancient sacrifice; in a third it has become the canon's dressing-room; indeed so changed are the destination of the rooms, so altered the characteristics and features of these residences, that were it not for a few feet of moulded stringcourse appearing occasionally on the cemented walls, an ornamented chimney stack, and a high pitched gable, they could scarcely be recognised as having once belonged to the ancient churchmen. What painful intrusions meet the eye at every turn in a cathedral close of the present time! one venerable building is converted into a finishing school for young ladies; another, with the blinds drawn down, is the residence of a dissenting minister; this vicar's house is a music shop, that a baker's; one canonry is let to some sporting gents; the deanery is shut up, and so are all the houses of those who are not on residence; or if unlet to lay intruders, these buildings exhibit only signs of habitation at long and distant periods, between which they remain as if hermetically closed: only when *the* canon is about leaving residence and *another* canon's time draws near, the shutters of a house suddenly are unclosed, windows are thrown open, and bedding hung out in the sun to air; sundry old women are seen either entering with pails and brooms, or in the act of cleaning; curtains are delivered from brown holland confinement, and looking-glass frames from gauze and paper coverings; fire-irons and polished grates are freed from grease, and brass ornaments affixed to the register fronts; stacks of chairs, sofas, and ottomans, are unpiled from the centre of the drawing-room, and disposed in tasteful variety round its confines; chimney ornaments and cut lustres resume their wonted station on the marble shelves. All is now ready, and in due time the whole party arrive; the canon and the canon's lady, the governess and the young canonesses, house-maids, kitchen-maids, lady's-maid, nursery-maids, and the complete modern ecclesiastical establishment; to remain three long months in this horribly dull old place, with the odious bell of the cathedral dismally sounding; and no relief except a few evening card parties and a juvenile ball.

means of a court left in the centre of the building, the whole is well lighted and ventilated. The entrance is from an arched doorway in Bath-street, communicating directly with a small cloister leading on the right towards the kitchen and offices, and on the left to the living and other rooms. On the ground floor are four chambers for priests, a chancery for the business of the district, and a strong room for muniments; and as by a distinct approach, housekeeper's and servants' rooms. In the basement are a waiting room, servants' hall, kitchen, scullery, cellars, larder and other offices. On the upper or principal floor, are, a common hall or dining room, communicating by a separate staircase with the kitchen, a private chapel, a library and two audience and sleeping chambers for the lord bishop and his right reverend coadjutor. Over these are four principal bed rooms, and eight cells for strangers. The annexed plate represents a view of the building taken from Bath-street; it will be seen that convenience has dictated the design, and that the elevation has been left in that natural irregularity produced by the internal arrangements, to which we owe the picturesque effect of the ancient buildings. The walls are built entirely of brick with stone dressings; and some ornamental devices are occasionally worked on the walls with vitrified bricks. At the corner of Weaman-street is an angle niche, containing an image of St. Chad standing on an angel corbel; the arms and initials of the Right Rev. Dr. Walsh are also introduced in tracery panels. The interior of both chapel and common hall are given in the same plate as the exterior view; in the former is a stained glass window with an image of St. Chad vested as he used to say mass, standing under a canopy, together with shields charged with his cross, and in the upper part of the window, many angels. The reredos of the altar is worked in stone gilt and paneled; it represents the Annunciation of our blessed Lady, in three niches and two compartments, as shown in the etching; the lower part of the altar is hung with a rich frontal of velvet and gold. On the Gospel side of the sanctuary is an almery for vestments; the altar is furnished with silk curtains, cross, candlesticks, and sacred vessels; and two exceedingly curious early German paintings, presented by the Earl of Shrewsbury, are fixed on each side of the altar window. The hall is capable of dining about sixty persons, and has a bay window and high dais at the upper end, and is protected from draughts by a glazed screen at the bottom. The fire place is of carved stone divided over the arch into three quatrefoils, with the arms of St. Chad, Bishop Walsh, and

Bishop Wiseman, surmounted by gilt mitres. The side windows are also filled with ornamented quarries, rich borders and arms, with the scriptures, *vigilandum*, and *omnia pro Christo*, running bendy. In the bay window, are the arms of the four new vicars-apostolic; and in the window, at the upper end, the arms of the present Queen, the Earl of Shrewsbury, and the late C. R. Blundell, of Ince, great benefactors to these buildings. Immediately over the screen at the bottom of the hall, and affixed to the wall, is a stone canopy, under which are three angels, bearing the arms of St. Chad, surmounted by a mitre, all richly painted and gilt, and very similar in arrangement to the arms formerly in the dining hall of the archiepiscopal palace at Croydon, Surrey; the tables, benches and other furniture of this hall are solidly framed and in perfect character with the style of the building. The library is a lofty room entirely surmounted with bookcases; the three windows are over these, and contain six shields of arms:— Bishop Walsh, Bishop Wiseman, the Earl of Shrewsbury, Mr. J. Hardman, St. Chad's, and St. Mary's, Oscott. The audience chambers are each provided with carved fireplaces, and oriel windows with emblems in stained glass, representing the holy name of our Lord illuminated, the emblems of the Passion, and a device illustrative of the most Holy Trinity, with appropriate scriptures. The remainder of the rooms contain nothing worthy of particular notice, and the rest of the building is fitted up with the most rigid simplicity. The cost of this edifice, including every expense, does not exceed £4,000, the stained glass and other decorations being contributed by benefactors; thus a residence which both in its ecclesiastical character and extent of accommodations, is in all respects suited for the occupation of the bishops and clergy, and also for transacting the increasing business of the district, has been erected for a sum which does not involve a greater annual outlay than would have been required for two large modern houses which must have been destitute of every requisite for this important purpose.

CONVENTS OF THE SISTERS OF MERCY AT BIRMINGHAM AND LIVERPOOL. (PLATE XII.)

Among the many important objects that have been lately accomplished by the English Catholics, the establishment of these charitable sisters is one which must prove most beneficial to the poorer classes and to the progress of religion in general. At London, Birmingham, and Liverpool, regu-

A prospect of the convent of our Lady of Mercy Birmingham

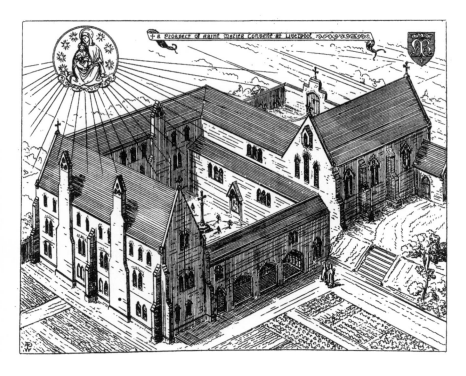

A prospect of Saint Maries Convent at Liverpool

lar communities are now formed, living in conventual buildings, and fulfilling all the sacred duties of the order with scrupulous exactitude. It is not our purpose to enlarge on the rule of these exemplary sisters, or the blessings and consolations that they are the means of imparting to the suffering population, these being matters which are generally understood. We will therefore turn at once to the consideration of the edifices that have been raised for the habitation of these sisterhoods, and which are the first regular conventual buildings erected in this country since the change of religion. The upper engraving represents the convent at Birmingham, lately completed; and the lower that about to be built at Liverpool. As the internal arrangement of both these houses will be essentially the same, it will be sufficient to describe that of Birmingham. This foundation owes its existence to the piety and munificence of Mr. John Hardman, sen., aided by a large grant from the Earl of Shrewsbury,—both great benefactors to the religious edifices lately erected in this town. The conventual buildings are constructed of bricks with stone doorways, windows, gables and dressings; and, as may be perceived by the engraving, the whole are extremely simple in design but yet of strictly ecclesiastical character; and from the unity of style which pervades the whole of this edifice, and which extends to the furniture and other fittings, it produces a striking illustration of the old religious houses, as they existed in all their regularity and order. The following is a list of the various chambers, &c. contained in this building;—chapel, cloisters, oratory, cemetery, sacristy, refectory, noviciate parlour, community room, work room for religious, twenty cells, school-room, dining room for poor children, dormitory and playing-room for ditto, kitchen and other offices. Within the chapel is a regular choir, containing twenty stalls, divided off by an open screen and rood from the ante-chapel. To the eastward of this is the sanctuary; the altar is of plain stone, with a frontal of silk, embroidered and ornamented with the Lamb, and emblems of the four evangelists; the reredos is of oak, with rich diapered panels, of various patterns; a pair of curtains are suspended on each side; and on the altar is a gilt tower for the reservation of the blessed Sacrament, and a pair of candlesticks. On either side of the east window, is an angel standing on a carved corbel and bearing a shield, charged with the five wounds of our Lord, and the emblems of the Passion. The roof is covered with inscriptions and ornaments in rich colours, the pattern consisting of quatrefoils, with the holy name connected by bands inscribed "mercy;" and round the upper parts of the walls "the angelical salutation" in illuminated letters. The floors of both choir and sanctuary are laid with figured tiles, charged with the armorial bearings of Lord Shrewsbury, and other appropriate devices: the east window, of three lights, is filled with stained glass, presented by the noble earl: in the middle day is an image of our blessed Lady, under a rich canopy; and on either side are effigies of the Earl of Shrewsbury and Mr. Hardman, as co-founders, in a kneeling attitude, attended by their patron saints. St. John the Baptist and St. John the Evangelist. The side windows of the choir are also filled with stained glass, of varied design and rich effect. This chapel is well furnished with sacred vessels and vestments, of a style corresponding to that of the building, and facsimiles to those used in England previous to the spoliation of the churches. A doorway on the north side of the lower end of the chapel leads into the cloisters, which are decorated by a succession of ancient images in niches, all richly diapered and painted according to their original colours; among these is the crucifixion of our Lord, with SS. Mary and John on a Calvary, St. Ann and our blessed Lady, St. Etheldreda, the wise men's offering, and the Annunciation of our blessed Lady. At the end of the north alley is an oratory with a stained window, and a large niche, containing the crucifixion of our Lord beautifully set forth in gold and colours, with a stone lantern for a lamp, by its side, similar to those remaining in the cloisters of Augsburg Cathedral; the space inclosed by these cloisters is consecrated for a cemetery with a floreated stone cross, raised on steps in the centre. This may be distinctly perceived by referring to the engraving, which will fully illustrate the external appearance and arrangement of the building. As the community rooms and cells have been finished in the simplest possible style, there is nothing farther to merit particular notice, except the absence of all those trifling ornaments and unworthy devotional emblems that sometimes disgrace the walls and shelves of modern convents, and which must have the effect of lessening in the minds of casual observers the respect that they would otherwise feel for their devout and exemplary inmates.

BENEDICTINE PRIORY OF ST. GREGORY'S, DOWNSIDE, NEAR BATH. (PLATE XIII.)

The next conventual building which we proceed to notice is one of a far more extended description, and of which a

tolerably correct idea may be formed from the accompanying view, which represents the whole edifice as complete. It is intended to erect so much of this design at present as the increasing wants of the community absolutely require, and to proceed with the remaining portions of the plan as means may admit. The building is an exact revival of one of the larger English monasteries: consisting of a church, great cloisters, with carrols for study, lavatory, and chapter-house, a refectory, with buttery, cellars and kitchens, calefactory, noviciate, library, dormitory, prior's lodgings, infirmary, and a chapel for the sick, with spacious offices and almonries, a strangers' court, with guest-rooms and hall, and a separate quadrangle for scholars, with class and lecture-rooms.

It is not many years since this community expended a considerable sum in the erection of a church, and other buildings; but these they found wholly inadequate to the present increasing wants; and being, moreover, deficient in solidity and convenience, it has been wisely determined to erect the new buildings so as to form part of a grand and perfect plan; in order that an edifice may be eventually completed in some degree worthy of this most venerable and famous order, to whom England is indebted for many of the most glorious monuments of ancient skill,—among which we can yet reckon the names of Westminster, Peterborough, Durham, and Gloucester, that have not been demolished for the repair of roads, or to satisfy the sacrilegious rapacity of court favourites.* The style adopted for this structure is early lancet,

---

* If Gloucester and Peterborough had not been converted into cathedral churches, they would doubtless have perished, like Glastonbury, Reading, Croyland, and many others, which were by no means inferior to them, either in extent, grandeur, or sacred associations. Westminster Abbey itself had a narrow escape from being levelled by the sacrilegious hands of the Protector Somerset, under Edward VI. Heylin says, " But the lord protector thinking it altogether unnecessary that two Cathedrals should be founded so near to one another, and thinking the church of Westminster (as being of a later foundation) might best be spared, had cast a longing eye on the goodly patrimony which remained unto it, and, being then unfurnshed of a house or palace proportionable to his greatness, he *doubted not to find room upon the dissolution and destruction of so large a fabrick* to raise a *palace equal to his vast design*, and he was only turned from the execution of this detestable project by the Dean, Benson, surrendering to him more than half the estates belonging to it. For this last act, coupled with his original surrender of the abbey, this wretched ecclesiastic was so tortured with remorse, that he died miserably a few months after. Tewkesbury abbey church, all glorious as it is with tombs and chapels of most surpassing interest and beauty, was also condemned to destruction, and only saved from immediate demolition by being purchased for a parochial church by the townsmen." The following entry respecting Tewkesbury abbey occurs in the account of the

as combining simplicity with true ecclesiastical character. Each alley of the cloister will measure above one hundred and fifty feet in length, the refectory eighty by thirty, the wall three and four feet thick; which may afford some data by which the extent and solidity of the buildings can be imagined. They will be constructed on the ancient principle of convenience and strength combined. without affectation of forced regularity and unnecessary features. Each portion of the edifice will bespeak its purpose, from the chapter-house to the kitchen. Roofs and chimney shafts stand forth undisguised in all the unadorned grandeur produced by their extent and solidity; and, when completed, this building will furnish an admirable proof of the vast superiority of effect that is produced by the *natural architecture of our Catholic ancestors mock-regularity system of modern builders.*

ST. BEDE'S MASBRO. (PLATE XIV).

We have great pleasure in introducing the accompanying views and plan of a small church, lately erected at Masbro, near Rotherham, under the superintendence of Mr. Matthew Hatfield. This may be regarded as an earnest of this gentleman's future intention of reviving true Catholic principles in such ecclesiastical buildings as he may be engaged to erect. It is indeed truly gratifying to see the rapid extension of correct ideas on these matters; for many earlier edifices raised by this architect were serious departures from the true Christian style, and we feel assured he will now be willing to admit the truth of this remark: but whatever errors of judgment he may formerly have committed, he now comes forward as a reviver of the true old school, and as such we hail him with unmingled satisfaction. On referring to the engraving, it will be perceived that all the essentials of a Catholic Church are included in the arrangement of this building.

---

suppression, and is truly characteristic of the spirit which introduced *what are now termed Anglo-Catholic principles.*

" Houses and buildings remaining undefaced.—The lodgings called the Newark, leading from the gate to the late abbot's lodgings, with *buttery, pantry, cellar, kitchen, larder,* and *pastry.* The abbot's lodgings, *stable, bakehouse, brewhouse* and *slaughterhouse, almery, barn, dairyhouse, maltinghouse, the oxhouse,* &c.

" Buildings deemed to be superfluous.—The *church, with chapels, cloister, chapterhouse, misericord;* the two *dormitories, infirmary, with chapels,* and lodging within the same, &c.

Thus, only a few cooking offices were thought worthy of being preserved of all this stupendous monastery, which, even its present delapidated and neglected state, fills every observer with admiration.

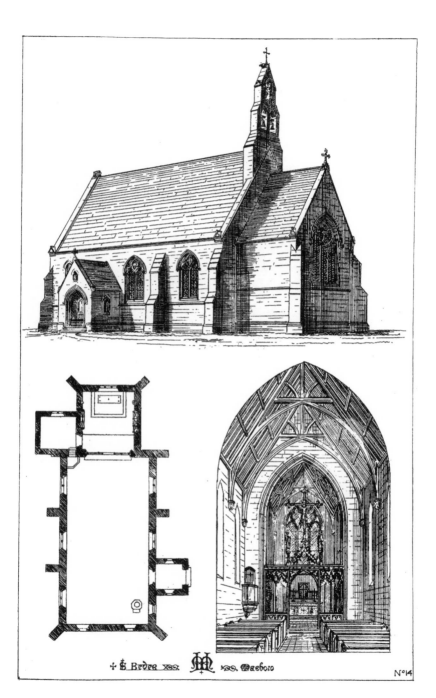

+ S. Bedes M. Maeboro

Nave, southern porch, font, chancel, rood screen, altar, sedilia, sepulchre, belfry, &c. ; and all those various features are designed in a correct style and in accordance with ancient models; and we trust that they will be fully carried out in execution, without curtailment or modification. As some persons have imagined that this building, from its striking resemblance to others lately erected under the superintendence of Mr. Pugin, must have been copied from them, it is only right, in justice to the architect, to say a few words on the subject. When buildings are derived from a common source, it it very natural that they should greatly resemble each other; hence, in the present revival of the Catholic architecture, the authorities for which can only be found in the ancient edifices of the country, it is very possible and even probable that two architects may erect precisely the same edifice; and this circumstance, *so far from being injurious to the reputation of either, is creditable to both.** We seek for *authority*, not *originality*, in these matters; for the establishment of *a principle, not individual celebrity*; and any man who possesses the true spirit of Christian art, so far from desiring to occupy an unrivalled position, is delighted when he is equalled, and overjoyed to be surpassed. It is far more gratifying to see a principle understood and practised by a number of persons, than for one man to enjoy an exclusive celebrity; and these are precisely the points which distinguish the Catholic from the Pagan artist. The former seek the glory of God and the Church; the latter the applause and admiration of men: the one is content to labour in accordance with the ancient traditions, from which he does not venture to deviate; the latter is perpetually seeking novelties, whereby he may attract attention and gain notoriety; hence all the horrible innovations introduced in the 16th century by the semi-pagan artists, who despised and rejected the

---

* Mr. Pugin, we believe, never claimed the least merit on the score of originality : nor does he profess to invent new combinations, but simply to revive, as far as circumstances and means will admit, the glorious but till lately despised works of the Middle Ages ; and no man can be more sensible of the great inferiority of the buildings he erects when compared with the original types from which they are derived; for although in the debased and degenerate age in which we live, the most trifling revival of better times seems a gigantic achievement, yet how insignificant do our greatest efforts appear, when compared with the works of Catholic antiquity; and although we may exult in the enthusiasm of the moment over the meagre imitations of ancient excellence which are being produced, yet, on mature consideration, and reference to the original types, we shall find them rather occasions for humiliation than for glory.

Catholic wisdom of centuries, that they might astonish for a season by their extravagances. These men, who sacrificed everything for a worldly triumph, were filled with envyings, jealousies, and detractions; but such vile passions, although natural to the Pagan courts of the Medici, found no place among the Catholic architects of the cloister, who, after raising the most glorious piles that ever emanated from the genius of man, wholly devoted to the *object* for which they laboured, have not even transmitted their names to posterity: and may we not hope that many artists will arise, as in days of old, to carry on the great work in the true spirit;—not in strife and contentions, not in prostitution of their art for the mere sake of gain;—not in pandering to the ignorance and whimsical fancies of those by whom they may chance to be employed;—but in a firm and uncompromising spirit revive Catholic art and architecture in all its integrity. If Mr. Pugin has been a somewhat successful restorer of ancient glory, he has attained the necessary knowledge by means which are open to all. He does not profess to hold any patent for the exercise of his art, nor to be in possession of hidden secrets, nor of any peculiar information that may not be obtained by patient study and research. Those who wish to attain excellence, *must distrust themselves, and become humble disciples of the old Catholic architects, whose silent teaching may be learnt from every venerable pile, from the humblest parish church to the vast and lofty cathedral;* and then, indeed, correct ideas and satisfactory buildings would soon become general, as in former times.

NEW CATHOLIC CHURCH AT ISLINGTON.

This church, so far from exhibiting the adoption of true Catholic principles, which we have had so much pleasure in describing at Masbro, is certainly the most original combination of modern deformity that has been erected for some time past for the sacred purpose of a Catholic church. It has been a fine opportunity thrown away; and the only consolation we can derive from its erection, is the hope that its palpable defects, by serving as an additional evidence of the absolute necessity of adhering to ancient Catholic examples in the churches we erect, may induce those in ecclesiastical authority to adopt this system in all cases, and to refuse their sanction to any modern experiments in ecclesiastical architecture. What renders the present case the more deplorable, is the fact that an ancient Catholic parochial church, dedicated in

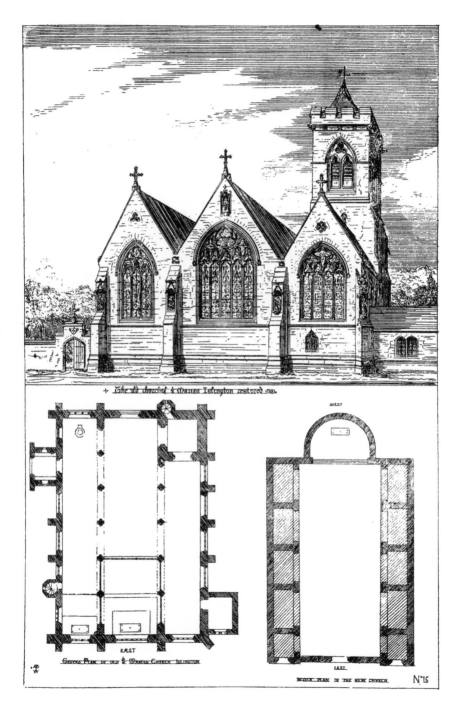

+ The old church of S. Maries Islington restored +

WEST

EAST

GROUND PLAN OF OLD S. MARIES CHURCH ISLINGTON

EAST

GROUND PLAN OF THE NEW CHURCH

Nº 16

honour of the Blessed Virgin, and in all respects suited to the present site and wants of the congregation, formerly existed at Islington, and was demolished only a few years since, to make room for the pewed and galleried assembly room which is at present used for the parochial Protestant service.

In the annexed plate (xv) we have given a view of this church as it would have appeared if erected on the site of the present building; in which case it would have stood in correct canonical position, due east and west, the high altar and side chapels facing the New River; while the tower, at the extremity of the north aisle, would have imparted the true character of a parochial church to the building, without encroaching on lateral space. By the plan, which is also given in the plate, it will be perceived that the high altar could be perfectly seen from all parts of the old church; which, strangely enough, was the reason advanced for departing from ancient arrangements, and confining the congregation to the mere nave of the present design, and blocking up the space which should have been occupied by the aisles, with cross walls.* See block plan of new church.

We are unwilling to attribute all the defects of this building to the architect, who has on former occasions shown himself capable of doing very much better, and who would be a valuable ally in the good cause, if he would seek to do what is positively right and correct, rather than what may please for the moment; and we fear he has been induced to arrange this building on the same principle that artists occasionally paint family portraits, out of all harmony and proportion,— so much pain, so much money. Yet surely this is quite unworthy of an ecclesiastical architect; these are not times for compromise; the English Catholics are no longer an obscure body, but stand as a light and a beacon to others who are on

---

* Some persons have pretended to justify this extraordinary arrangement of cross walls, by alleging that glorious example of ancient art, King's College Chapel at Cambridge; but independently of the manifest absurdity of selecting an example of the latter pointed architecture as any authority for an edifice which by its round-headed arches is evidently intended as an imitation of the Norman style, every one acquainted with the chapel of King's must be aware that the lateral chapels were suggested by the enormous projection of the buttresses, which were *absolutely necessary* to *resist the lateral thrust of the flattened groined ceiling of massive masonry*. But at Islington, so far from any thing like groining, there is an open truss roof without any thrust at all; and instead of the cross walls being required as buttresses, they are not carried up higher than the bottom of the clerestory, so that in fact they answer no other end than to block up the space which should be open for aisles, and to reduce the accommodation of the church by nearly one-half.

all sides seeking the truth; they are at the present time in a fearful state of responsibility, and sad it is indeed that by the erection of this, or similar departures from true Catholic architecture, they should afford a temporary triumph to the infidels. The Church at Islington is built on the *all front principle* of Dissenters, and is by no means equal to the Puritan edition of York Minster at the Scotch Kirk, Regent-square, though it likewise apes two diminutive towers at the west end of a church which is neither collegiate, conventual, nor cathedral. The united cost of these would have erected a good massive parochial tower at the western end. Indeed this building is in all respects so painful a subject, that it would not have been introduced at all, if the exposure of error did not contribute greatly to the advancement of truth; and in the present case it seems absolutely necessary to demonstrate the fallacy of the principle which instigated its extraordinary arrangement, and to set forth the great superiority which aisled Churches possess, in every respect, over large rooms, which some persons in these days advocate strongly as the best form for religious structures.

The annexed plate (xvi) represents the section and plan of one compartment of a large assembly room, quite square, with a flat ceiling, shown by the walls lightly tinted; and a Catholic Church, with nave and aisles, indicated by the dark plan and walls.

By this engraving it will be seen, that a mere room of fifty feet in width, if it possess requisite strength of walls and timber of sufficient scantling to bear a flat truss for such a span, will require considerably more material, both for walling and roof, than a church with aisles of sixty or even seventy feet wide in the clear, on account of the subdivision of the roof into three parts. Few persons are aware of the vast expense attendant on the erection of large rooms; the mere cost of hoisting principals of fifty feet wide into their places would cover that of fixing the roofs on an aisled Church complete, while the *ornamental plaster ceiling* that is required to hide the flat-framed roofs of these modern rooms would literally furnish an ordinary Church with altars, stained glass, and fittings. Hence, by adhering to the old Catholic method of Church building, we have an increased width of ten to twenty feet, a great saving of materials and expense, and a most solemn and impressive effect produced upon the mind. Aisle roofs act as buttresses without obstruction. Islington Church is *only a nave after all;* if it had aisles, all the people who

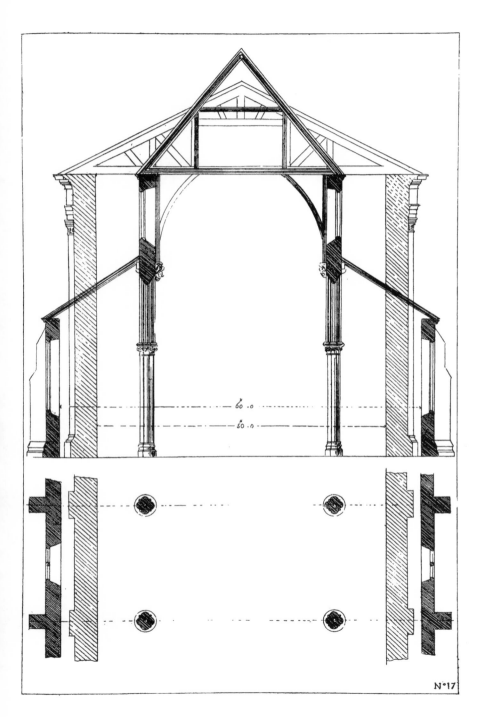

N°17

are at present accommodated would not be inconvenienced, and half as many more would be nearly as well located even on the score of seeing the altar; for the pillars in the naves of the old parochial churches are but very slight obstructions.

But increase of space, coupled with economy, is not the only reason for the superiority of the aisle arrangement. *A large square room is the worst possible form for the conveyance of sound*; and the voice of the same individual that can be distinctly heard in a large church subdivided by pillars, would be utterly lost in an unbroken space of considerably less extent. It will now be seen that the superiority of the Catholic over the modern or Pagan form of a church, can be demonstrated for the soundest practical reasons : as for mystical ones, they are so evident as scarcely to need any notice. All the associations of aisles are Catholic; the very word itself conjures up to our minds solemn processions, long and tapering perspectives, monastic grandeur, and heavenly chants; they form, in fact, after the chancel, the most striking external characteristic which distinguishes the temple of God from a common assembly room, the church from the conventicle; and most earnestly do we hope, that these most essential portions of a true Catholic church will never again be omitted, for the sake of substituting a set of unsightly recesses, not very dissimilar from those lately erected under the Greenwich and Blackwall railways, or the divisions technically termed wing-rooms, which serve as depositories for scenery on the stages of the metropolitan theatres.

In a former part of this article we have endeavoured to render all possible justice to the able advocacy of Catholic architecture and antiquities by certain learned writers of the Anglican Church. While doing this we felt it necessary to allude occasionally to certain inconsistencies and erroneous statements which are found in these publications.* We now

---

* In the " Christian Remembrancer" of a few months since, we noticed some remarks on an article treating on ecclesiastical architecture (that had appeared in this Review), which were conceived in the most anti-catholic spirit, although the writer at the same time appeared very anxious to be considered as one of the faithful. He evidently belongs to that class of persons who assume the title of Catholic as a *nom de guerre*, the better to forward certain heretical designs in which they are engaged, and while professing to revive truth and antiquity, are proved by their very writings to be the promulgators of dangerous errors and foolish conceits. The assertions of the writer in question are made with so much confidence, and have at the same time so little foundation in truth, that it becomes a duty to expose the errors and inconsistencies into which he has fallen. In the first place, he attributes to *mere inadvertence* the passages which refer to the lingering love of ancient architecture that partially existed

purpose to show wherein these consist, and to prove that, excellent as are the principles advanced in these writings, they are

---

in England after the change of religion. Now, so far from these accounts being unguarded admissions, they were sober testimonies, made with much satisfaction, and referred to authorities; and there is not one passage of the article in question that can possibly deserve the accusation of disingenuousness. The writer in the " Christian Remembrancer " does not appear to possess much candour or sincerity; he states a few isolated facts, and makes general deductions from them, and not unfrequently perverts the true meaning of the statements themselves. He first attempts to prove the continuance of Catholic rites in the present Anglican church, from the fact of some old candlesticks being occasionally mentioned in church inventories, which he is obliged to confess are not used for lights; and then farther on he argues against the use of lights at all, by perverting the obvious meaning of a passage in the " Review." Respecting the communion plate, which he speaks of in the better sort of parish churches, the reviewer has had ample opportunity of inspecting the same, and a viler collection of misshapen vessels are not to be found in Christendom; goblet-shaped chalices, huge flagons, somewhat resembling black jacks, spreading salvers, without one vestige or type of Catholic antiquity about them; and as for candlesticks, they may be occasionally found, but void of tapers or lights; for, as the Anglo-German father, Bucer, says of candles,

> " Their use for ornament
> On God's board may be innocent,
> *But do not light them as on stages,*
> *So may two candles last for ages,*
> *Yet better 'twere you used none*
> *For shunning superstition."*

And this latter advice is generally observed; for, notwithstanding the boastings of this writer, it would be scarcely possible for him to point out one church in the occupation of the Establishment, where lights are used during the celebration of the communion service, unless the impenetrable obscurity of a London fog might haply serve as reasonable excuse for reviving this Anglo-Catholic practice on a solitary occasion. The only instance where lights were attempted to be used on the old mystical principles in these latter times, was speedily followed by an injunction from the bishop for the immediate removal of candlesticks and all Popish ornaments out of the chancel. While we are on this subject, it may be proper to mention the egregious mistake into which the writer has fallen respecting the antiquity of the mystical use of lights in the church : it was mentioned in the review, that lights were not placed *on the altar* previous to the 10th century; but in the concluding part of the passage it stated *where they were disposed, round the altar, in coronas, on the rood beams in suspended lamps,* &c.; but this latter portion, not suiting his object, he leaves unnoticed, and exclaims in exultation, " So, if we have no lights at all, we are following the primitive usage; for it is admitted there were no candles on the altar in the early church;" and he adds, in a note, that Durandus, who wrote in the beginning of the 13th century, speaks only of one candelabrum, and which he does not describe, as on the altar; and that in the church of St. Clement, at Rome, this candelabrum was in *the choir adjoining one of the pulpits.* Now it is by no means surprising that a man, who has been both educated a Protestant, and remains a member of a Protestant communion, possessing but meagre sources for information on these matters, should fall into great mistakes; but it is astonishing that any one so utterly deficient in the ordinary knowledge of ecclesiastical antiquities, can so boldly advance such untenable positions. Durandus, so far from confining his account of lights to one candelabrum, has devoted a whole chapter to the subject, divided under five heads; the first of

frequently advocated on *false and untenable grounds.* In doing this we shall probably offend many whose goodwill we should

---

which is as follows: " Candelabrorum et lucernarum *usus antiquissimus.*" In every liturgical writer of any note, this subject is explained and illustrated at great length, and in a most satisfactory and conclusive manner.

Respecting the one candelabrum at St. Clement's church, it is neither more nor less than the pascal candlestick for the great candle lighted at Easter ; which in many of the Roman churches is a *fixture on the gospel side of the choir, which is its correct position ;* and it was placed adjacent to one of the pulpits, not for the purpose of affording light to a reader, as the italics of the writer would seem to imply, but for the greater convenience of the deacon, who during the chanting of the hymn " Exultat," has to infix five grains of incense in the candle, and also attach the pascal table, or list of moveable feasts, and other ecclesiastical matters, to it. As the candle is in itself generally of a considerable size, with a corresponding pedestal, the deacon is necessarily obliged to ascend a fixed or moveable pulpit for these purposes ; hence the position of the candelabrum at St. Clement's. In D'Agincourt's great work on art, there are three representations of such pascal candlesticks, by pulpits or ambones, with the deacon ; and in " Gerberti de Cantu et Musica Sacra a prima Ecclesiæ ætate usque ad præsens tempus," a very curious representation of the tenth century is given, of a pascal candlestick rich in ornament, close to an ambo or pulpit, in which the deacon is figured in the act of affixing the pascal table to the candle. It is impossible to have more conclusive proof of the real intention of these candelabra, and the absurdity of the deductions which the writer in the " Remembrancer" has attempted to draw from them. His observations respecting vestments betray equal ignorance ; he evidently confounds the alb with the surplice, and the cope with the chasuble. The English surplice is, in fact, the Roman one ; it may be seen figured in every plate of the Roman pontifical, is still used in that city, and worn by a great portion of the English Catholic clergy, at the present day ; and the crimped surplices were only partially introduced in this country in consequence of the English Catholics being driven by the severity of penal laws to seek education in France ; as this Anglo-*Catholic* state at that time obliged every man to swear himself a *Protestant, or lose his lands, liberty, and even life :* but these, like other temporary innovations consequent on Protestant ascendency, are rapidly disappearing with the revival of ancient solemnity.

Albs are not crimped or curtailed, but, several of the modern ones are flounced, and are vastly similar in style to ladies' dresses. Albs of the ancient form, and *apparelled in precisely the same manner as those which belonged to the old English churches previous to the reign of Edward the Sixth,* have been revived in many places ; while they are utterly disused by the members of the Establishment, who certainly have little room for reproaching others with any neglect or departures in these respects, since of all the ancient vestments they have retained nothing but the surplice—*which is not by any means a distinguishing habit for the priestly office :* and this, open in front, and hastily adjusted over a fashionably cut coat, tight pantaloons, and a modern cravat, fails to convey the least resemblance of an ecclesiastic of the olden time. As regarding copes, which this writer strangely confounds with vestments or chasubles, they have never experienced any alteration whatever in form, and those used by the English Catholic clergy at the present time are precisely similar in shape and make to those used before the change of religion ; while the copes cited by the writer as worn at the coronations, are for the most part strange departures from ancient authority.

The chasuble has been terribly clipped in modern times of its original ample form, but it has lately regained much of its former dignity ; indeed no one would attempt to deny that poverty and bad taste combined have curtailed the

be anxious to retain, but the cause of Catholic truth is too sacred to admit of our acquiescing in false views on the score of expediency, or from the hope of obtaining certain ends which would seem to be better advanced by following such a course. We purpose, therefore, to set forth from the most authentic sources the real history of the disasters that have fallen on our sacred edifices since the sixteenth century; and this has

---

sacred vestments of half their ancient splendour, but still *the principle has never been abandoned by the English Catholics even under the most trying circumstances.* The clergy were compelled at one time to carry the vestments rolled into as small a compass as possible, from house to house, where they administered the consolations of religion to the scattered faithful : they were mean, they were ugly, *but there were the things; no priest ventured to celebrate without them, or without repeating the solemn prayers ordered by the Church while vesting.* Thus the traditions of England have been preserved by a few proscribed and persecuted Catholics, while the Anglicans have lost every vestige of ancient dignity; and at this moment the former are restoring the rites of the old religion in all their solemnity, while the latter *dare not even adhere to the trifling ornament allowed by the rubric;* but vestments, altars, and lights, are at complete variance with the *spirit of the present system.* Its founders abolished them altogether; they were partially revived through the whim of the tyrant Elizabeth, and the terrified puritans and irreverent dissenters, whom she introduced into the English bishoprics, consented to disguise themselves awhile in copes and surplices, the readier to infuse their pestilent doctrines among the people; for such are the reasons urged for their compliance by the foreign Protestants whom they consulted. (See Strype.) These relics of the old Church were rapidly dying away, when Laud attempted to stem the tide of Protestantism, but in vain; and copes, bishops, and king, fell victims to the Protestant principles that had so long been fostered among the people. Whatever might have been the efforts of a few Catholic-minded men at the restoration, the *glorious revolution* utterly extinguished all hopes of better things; and since that time Anglo-Protestantism has appeared as bare, meagre, and irreverent as its first concoctors and Genevan fathers could possibly desire.

We have gone at length into these remarks, because the writer in the "Christian Remembrancer" represents a most subtle and dangerous section existing in the Anglican Church; who by pushing forward the opinions of certain isolated writers, exceptions to the rule, and condemned by their cotemporaries as favourers of popery, are endeavouring to claim for the transactions of the Anglican Church for the last three centuries, a character which it is impossible on true grounds to substantiate. These men would affect Catholic rites, without possessing one particle of Catholic feeling or principle; they would fain enjoy the estate without fulfilling the tenure by which it must be held, and would assume the externals of antiquity the better to delude the people. But copes and two candlesticks are not the test of Catholicism; and if these persons did even figure for a while in the lion's skin they would soon betray the ass underneath, and only succeed in disgusting the Protestants with whom they associate, without either gaining grace, or advancing one step towards extricating themselves from the tangles of heresy which enthral them. These men of proud and obdurate hearts must not be confounded with those devout souls yet in the communion of the Anglican Church, who in austerities, mortifications, and humble piety, are seriously seeking the truth, and whose works and lives breathe the spirit of holiness and the feelings of ancient and better times. Humility, combined with an earnest desire of unity and truth, must be rewarded with the Divine blessing; but insolent and unfounded pretensions can only tend to promote the anger of the Almighty, and the ridicule and indignation of men.

become the more necessary, as doubtless there are many sincere men who write on these subjects *rather as they hope and wish than from actual research*, and are but little acquainted with the real state of the case, or the direful sacrilege that has been perpetrated under the system they extol. Far be it from us to charge the present race of Anglican clergy with any participation, by approval or otherwise, in the guilt of these enormities, or to hold them as answerable for sins of which our common fathers were guilty; indeed their works and writings for the most part prove them to possess a far different and better spirit: but our present object is to show the great inconsistency, or rather (to speak more properly) the impossibility of maintaining the principles which they now advocate on any but the ancient grounds; and the absurdity of claiming Catholic practices as belonging to the present system, which have in fact been abolished from its very commencement, and the very idea of which is a perfect novelty among the Anglicans themselves. That learned and reflecting men should be utterly disgusted with the meagre worship and Protestantism of the establishment, is natural, and at the same time gratifying; but they should endeavour to draw reasonable and legitimate conclusions from their convictions, and not put forth an imaginary Catholic system, and endeavour to throw the whole odium of Church plunder and desecration on the Puritan faction during the civil wars, who, after all, had but a comparatively small share in the execrable work. It does also seem most inconsistent, that those who have fallen to the lowest ebb in ecclesiastical rites and observances, and who have been as yet unable to extricate themselves from their degraded position, should assail in no very measured terms of reproach and insult, the English Catholic body; who, although far from exhibiting a standard of Catholic perfection, have retained the light of the old faith through a long series of bitter trials; and, with all the disadvantages under which they labour, are practically restoring at the present hour the very glories which their defamers can advocate only in theory.

With respect to the Puritans under Cromwell, so far from their being the great instrument for the destruction of England's glorious churches, these were defaced, plundered, and desecrated from the commencement of the so-called Reformation; and the ravages of the Cromwellian faction, execrable as they were, can by no means be compared to the sacrilegious outrages which preceded them, under the *direct sanction of the leading schismatics during the reigns of Henry the Eighth, Ed-*

ward the Sixth, and Elizabeth. It is now become a habit with
Anglican writers to talk very largely about the demolitions of
the seventeenth century; but when these accounts are tested
by historical documents, we shall find the second Cromwell
bleaches by the side of his more ancient namesake;—he certainly demolished many curious castellated mansions; and some
ecclesiastical buildings suffered no little damage by shot and
outrage; but it would be difficult to prove that he consigned
one noble church to wilful destruction; while, during the reign
of Henry, many of the *very finest* churches in Christendom
were barbarously destroyed for the mere material, and scarcely
a stone of them left standing: and how can the tossing over of
a few communion tables, of mean material and vile design, be
compared to the entire plunder and demolition of the ancient
altars, consecrated by our most holy prelates, and on many of
which the eucharistic sacrifice had been offered up, almost from
the planting of the faith itself in the land?—altars sparkling
with jewels, rich with gold, marbles, and enamels, exquisite in
design, and whose precious frontals were but types of the more
precious relics of God's holy saints that lay enshrined beneath
them; and those gems and rich offerings were plundered, and
those sacred relics scattered, and those consecrated stones, on
which the holy bishops of old had poured out the sacred oil,
split, and laid as paving for the infidels to trample on. And this,
not by Puritans of the seventeenth, but of the sixteenth century,
by that *arch apostate, the father of Puritans and modern Anglicans, Cranmer and his Zuinglian associates, whom he introduced
and fostered to blaspheme and profane the saintly ecclesiastics
and churches of our land.* Roundhead troopers had found
nought to steal but a few mean copes and surplices; royal commissioners had long before cleared out the oaken almeries that
lined the vaulted sacristies of old,—they were plundered of their
costly contents by kingly robbers of an older date. Jewelled
mitres, copes and vestments of golden tissue, orphreys of pearls,
and curious silken imagery, were considered as Popish superstitions by Anglican fathers, and very *meet for regal use.* When
were the shrines of Bede the venerable, the saintly Hugh of
Lincoln, St. Cuthbert of Durham, St. Guthlae of Croyland,
St. Chad of Lichfield, St. Swithun of Winchester, St. Thomas
of Canterbury, and St. Alban, England's protomartyr, with
hosts of others, seized and destroyed?—not by Puritans, but by
English schismatics, who, having basely sold their birthright
to a tyrant, denied their faith, renounced their spiritual alle-

giance to Christ's vicar, and became by the punishment of God the witnesses and instruments of their own shame. When did Canterbury's vaulted crypt, where holy prelates lie entombed, first echo with Huguenot preachers? *—when were those solemn piles, that faithful Englishmen had reared to God, desecrated by Walloon and Dutch ministers.† The Catholic structures were never more defiled in *Barebones'* days than this, —yet such were the motley crews welcomed by the innovators to assist in poisoning the minds and faith of the people.

The Puritans of Cromwell's time did but work out the principles of what is termed England's Reformation; there is not, in fact, one act of horrible sacrilege, contempt of ecclesiastical authority, or desecration of holy things and places, of which the Puritans were guilty, that had not been perpetrated ten times over, and under far more aggravated circumstances, by those who first reduced the English Church to her wretched state of schism and temporal bondage. Let our holy and just indignation fall on the truly guilty. Let us go at once to the *source of the evil, and assail the root, and condemn the betrayers rather than the betrayed.* We can even feel compassion and sorrow for the poor, ignorant, and misled fanatic of the latter times; but we will contend, with loud and lasting denunciations against the *authors of the lamentable evil,—those apostate bishops who betrayed the Church of which they were the unworthy pastors; who first abolished sacrifice, destroyed the altars of God, violated the sanctuaries, and instilled those principles of irreverence and infidelity into the minds of the people,* which, from that fatal period, have always lain smouldering and unextinguished, and from time to time break forth in open outrages;—of which the Cromwellian rebellion is but a fearful example. We will now proceed to bring forward historical documents in support of our positions.

OF THE DESTRUCTION OF ALTARS.

The destruction and desecration of altars during the reign of Henry must have been very extensive, owing to the vast

---

* A portion of the crypt at Canterbury was assigned for a French Protestant church, shortly after the establishment of Protestantism. See Hasted's "Canterbury Cathedral."

† The Austin Friars, in London, was given to the Dutch Protestants as a preaching place; it was once a most glorious church. Stow, who remembered it in its glory, describes it thus: "A large church, having a most fine spired steeple, small, high, and straight, *so that I have not seen the like.* But that goodly steeple, and all the eastern end, hath been lately taken down for one man's commodity," &c.

number of the most spacious and splendid churches belonging
to religious houses, which were demolished immediately after
the suppression of the monastic establishments; and among
these were probably some of the richest in the country : but
it does not appear that any altars in parochial, collegiate or
cathedral churches, were either destroyed or plundered to any
great extent till the succeeding reign of Edward the Sixth,
when the Protestantism of the so-called reformers was fully
developed; and Cranmer, who during the life of Henry had
outwardly conformed to the old rites, ceased to dissemble his
real opinions, and, urged by the instigations of the Calvinist
and Zuinglian faction, soon stripped the English Church of
her ancient solemnity, and rendered her, both in externals
and ritual, as bare and meager as the Genevan heretics of the
day could possibly desire.

In the account of the coronation of King Edward the
Sixth, given in *Strype's Memorials of Cranmer*, p. 142, the
high altar of Westminster is described as richly garnished
with divers and costly jewels and ornaments, of much esti-
mation and value; and also the tombs on each side of the high
altar, richly hanged with fine gold arras. Cranmer himself
also appeared on this occasion in the ancient archiepiscopal
vestments ; for we read in the same account, that at nine of
the clock all Westminster choir was in their copes, and three
goodly crosses before them: and after them other three goodly
rich crosses, and the king's chapel, with his children following,
all in scarlet, with surplices and copes on their backs; and
after them ten bishops in scarlet, with their rochets and rich
copes on their backs, and their mitres on their heads, did set
forth at the west door of Westminster, towards the king's
palace, there to receive his grace; *and my Lord of Canterbury,
with his cross before him, alone, and his mitre on his head.*
Such were the solemnities retained in the English Church in
1546, after the reign of such a destructive tyrant as Henry ;
but the Genevan emissaries had not yet arrived to extinguish
the fading light of England's ancient glory; for, after their
ever-to-be-detested presence, under the protection of Cranmer,—(who having betrayed the Church to the merciless tyranny of the state, introduced these wretched foreigners to
complete the havoc, and annihilate the faith), so rapid were
the strides of sacrilege and irreverence, that within four years
of the event just described at Westminster, *scarcely one altar
was left standing or unpillaged throughout the whole land ;* and
soon after, the very ornaments which decorated the altar on

the solemnity of the coronation, were conveyed away from the church by the authorized robbers of the day.*

1550 was the eventful year in which the destruction of those altars, on which the English clergy had offered up the holy sacrifice for so many centuries, were defaced and overthrown. Heylin's account of the proceedings is so very important, that it is here given at length.

" But the great business of this year was the taking down of altars, in many places by the public authority ; which in some few had formerly been pulled down by the irregular forwardness of the common people. The principal motive whereunto was, *in the first place, the opinion of some dislikes, which had been taken by Calvin against the Liturgy ; and the desire of those of the Zuinglian faction to reduce this church unto the nakedness and simplicity of those transmarine churches which followed the Helvetian or Calvinian forms.* For the advancement of which work, it had been preached by Hooper, above-mentioned, before the king about the beginning of this year,—that it would be very well, that it might please the magistrates to turn the altars into tables, according to the first institution of Christ ; and thereby to take away the false persuasion of the people, which they have of sacrifices to be done upon the altars. Because (saith he) as long as altars remain, both the ignorant people and the ignorant and evil persuaded priest, will dream always of sacrifice. This was enough to put the thoughts of the alteration into the heads of some great men about the Court, who thereby promised themselves no small hopes of profit by the disfurnishing of the altars, of the hangings, pales, plate and other rich utensils, which every parish, more or less, had provided for them. And that this consideration might prevail upon them as much as any other, if perhaps not more, may be collected from an inquiry made about two years after, in which it was to be interrogated, what jewels of gold and silver, or silver crosses, candlesticks, censors, chalices, copes, and other vestments, were then remaining in any of the cathedral or parochial churches ; or otherwise had been embezzled or taken away ; the leaving of one chalice to

---

* Heylin, p. 133. " That in pursuance of the faculties and instructions wherewith the king's commissioners were empowered...on May the 9th, 1553, Sir Roger Chomley, knight, lord chief justice, and Sir Robert Bowes, knight, master of the rolls, the king's commissioners for gathering ecclesiastical goods, held their session at Westminster, and called before them the dean of that cathedral, and certain others of the same house, and commanded them by virtue of the commission, to bring to them a true inventory of all the plate, cups, vestments, and other ecclesiastical goods which belonged to the church; which goods, the 12th day of the same month, were delivered to the said collectors ; *who left no more unto the Church than two cups with the covers gilt, and one white silver pot, with a few carpets, cushions, and hearse-cloths ! !*"

every church, with a cloth or covering for the communion table, being thought sufficient.

"The matter being thus resolved on, a letter comes to bishop Ridley, in the name of the king, *signed with his royal signet, but subscribed by Somerset, and other of the Lords of the Council,* concerning the taking down of altars and setting up tables in the stead thereof : which letter, because it relates to somewhat which was done before, in some of the churches, and seems only to pretend to an uniformity in all the rest, I shall here subjoin, that being the chief ground on which so great an alteration must be supposed to have been raised. Now the tenour of the said letter is as followeth :

"Right Reverend Father in God, right trusty and well beloved, we greet you well : whereas it is come to our knowledge, that, being the altars within the more part of the churches of the realm, upon good and godly considerations, are taken down, there doth yet remain altars standing in divers other churches ; by occasion whereof much variance and contention ariseth among sundry of our subjects, which, if good foresight we had not, might perhaps engender great hurt and inconvenience. We let you wit, that minding to have all occasions of contentions taken away, which many times groweth by those and such like diversities ; and considering, that amongst other things belonging to our royal office and care, we do account the greatest to be to maintain the common quiet of our realm ; we have thought good, by the advice of our council, to require you, and nevertheless especially to charge and command you, for the avoiding of all matters of further contention and strife about the standing or taking away of the said altars, to give substantial order through all your diocese ; that with all diligence, all the altars in every church or chapel, as well in places exempted as not exempted, within your said diocese, be taken down, and instead of them a table to be set up in some convenient part of the chancel within every such church or chapel, to serve for the ministration of the blessed communion. And, to the intent the same may be done without the offence of such of our loving subjects as be not yet so well persuaded in that behalf as we could wish, we send unto you herewith certain considerations, gathered and collected, that make for the purpose. The which and such others as you shall think meet, to be set forth to persuade the weak to embrace our proceedings in this part, we pray you cause to be declared to the people by some discreet preachers in such places as you shall think meet, before the taking down of the said altars, so as both the weak consciences of others may be instructed and satisfied as much as may be ; and this our pleasure the more quietly executed. For the better doing whereof we require you to open the foresaid considerations, in that our cathedral church, in your own person if you conveniently may, or otherwise by your chancellor or other grave preacher, both there and in such other market towns and most notable places of your diocese, as you may think most requisite.

" Which letter, bearing date on the 24th of November, in the fourth year of the king, was subscribed by the Duke of Somerset, the Archbishop of Canterbury, the lord Admiral Clinton, the Earls of Warwick, Bedford, and Wiltshire ; the Bishop of Ely, the Lords Wentworth and North.

" Now the effect of the said reasons mentioned in the last part of this letter, were, first, to move the people from the superstitious opinions of the people of the Popish mass unto the right use of the Lord's Supper ; *the use of an altar being to sacrifice upon, and the use of a table to eat upon* ; and therefore a table to be far more fit for our feeding on him, who was once only crucified and offered for us. Secondly, that in the *Book of the Common Prayer*, the name of altar, the Lord's board, and table, are used indifferently, without prescribing anything in the form thereof. For as it is called a table, and the Lord's board, in reference to the Lord's Supper, which is there administered, so it is called an altar also, in reference to the sacrifice of praise and thanksgiving, which is there offered unto God. And so the changing the altars into tables not to be any way repugnant to the rules of the Liturgy. The third reason seems to be no other than an illustration of the first, for taking away the superstitious opinion out of the minds of the people touching the sacrifice of the mass, which was not to be celebrated but upon an altar. The fourth, that the altars were erected for the sacrifices of the law, which being now ceased, the form of the altar was to cease together with them. The fifth, that as Christ did institute the sacrament of his body and blood at a table, and not at an altar (as it appeareth by the three Evangelists), so it is not to be found that any of the Apostles did ever use an altar in the ministration. And finally, that it is declared in the preface to the *Book of Common Prayer*, that if any doubt arise in the use and practising of the said book, that then, to appease all such diversity, the matter shall be referred unto the bishop of the diocese, who by his discretion shall take order for the quieting of it.

" The letter, with these reasons, being brought to Ridley, there was no time for him to dispute the commands of the one, or to examine the validity and strength of the other. And thereupon proceeding shortly after to his first visitation, he gave out one injunction, amongst others, to this effect, that those churches in his diocese, where the altars do remain, shall conform themselves unto those other churches which had taken them down ; and that instead of the multitude of their altars they should set up one decent table in every Church. But this being done, a question afterwards did arise about the form of the Lord's board, some using it in the form of a table, and others in the form of an altar : which being referred unto the determination of the bishop, he declared himself in favour of that posture or position of it, which he conceived most likely to procure an uniformity in all his diocese, and to be more agreeably to the king's godly proceedings, in abolishing divers vain and superstitious opinions about the mass out of the hearts of the people. Upon which declaration, or determination, he appointed the form of a right table to be used in his diocese; and caused the wall standing on the back side of the altar, in the Church of St. Paul's, to be broken down for an example to the rest. And being thus a leading case to all the rest of the kingdom, it was followed, either with a swifter or a slower pace, according as the bishops in their several dioceses, or the clergy in their several parishes, stood affected to it. No universal change of altars into tables, in all parts of the realm, till the repealing of the first liturgy, in which the priest is appointed to stand before the middest of the altar in the celebration; and the establishing of the second, in which it is required that the priest shall stand on the north side of the table, had put an end to the dispute."

From this account we may gather the following important facts :—

1st. That Calvin and the Zuinglians were the authors of this detestable sacrilege.

2d. That excepting Cranmer and a few apostates of the same class, the English clergy had no part in the foul deed.

3d. That the order proceeded from lay authorities.

4th. That the object of these lay authorities was plunder of church ornaments.

5th. That the reason assigned by Cranmer and the Protestant clergy for the demolition was, in order to *abolish the idea of sacrifice.*

6th. That the destruction of the ancient altars must be referred to this period, and not to the Puritanic rebellion under Cromwell.

Refusal to desecrate the altars of God, was considered a sufficient cause for depriving a bishop of his see: for we are informed by Strype (Cranmer, p. 228), that Bishop Hethe, of Worcester, came before the "council, and being asked *what he said to the letters sent to him from the king's majesty,* he answered, that he could not conform *his conscience to take down altars in the churches,* and in lieu of them to set up tables as the letter appointed; alleging further, that Scripture and the fathers were in their favour." Cranmer and Ridley both endeavoured to dissuade the bishop from his opinion, but without effect.

Four days after, Bishop Day, of Chichester, was summoned on

the same account, and remanded till the 7th, when he answered plainly he could not comply in conscience with the injunctions of the *king's letter;* for the "altars seemed to him a thing anciently established by the agreement of the holy fathers, and confirmed by the ancient doctors, with the custom also of a number of years, and as he thought according to the Scriptures; wherefore he could not consent to the abolishing of them, and determined rather to lose all that he ever had than to condemn his own conscience." Whereupon, Strype adds, for his contempt, he was committed by order of the council; so we hear no more of him and his fellow the bishop of Worcester, till nine months hence; *so we leave them in the Fleet.* At the expiration of that time they were both deposed, and the Puritan Hooper was introduced into Worcester, to make havoc of that glorious Church, and to deface it, in the same manner as he had previously done at Gloucester; Scory, of Rochester, was nominated to Chichester.*

We find in Dugdale's History of St. Paul's, that in the 7th year of king Edward the Sixth, the dean and chapter of that church petitioned for an allowance of £28. 6s. 4d. towards their expenses *in taking down the steps and place of the high altar,* and other alterations. From this item it will be see that *Dowsing's* proceedings in the reign of Cromwell were quite in the true Protestant spirit of the reformed Anglican Church; for he ordered chancel steps to be levelled, which was done by the mother church of London a century previous. Not content with demolishing altars, it was customary to lay down the consecrated slab *as a common paving-stone,* in which position many still remain at Lincoln Minster, and other places.

The parish accounts of this period furnish most interesting particulars respecting the sale of altars, which were made into lots.

	s.	d.
" St. Lawrence's Church, Reading, 1551.		
Received of Mr. Grey for St John's altar and *the cope chest*	6	8
Received of Mr. Grey, for the Trinitie altar of marble, with the trimming	10	8

---

* Thus were the sacrilegious destructions, termed in our days *Anglo-Catholic reforms,* carried on by an apostate archbishop and some plundering courtiers ; and if any ecclesiastics dared to resist the usurped power and defend the ancient customs of the Church, they were imprisoned and deposed, to make room for Puritanic intruders, fresh from Frankfort or Geneva, and ready for any work of savage fanaticism.

I

Received of Mr. Buckland for Jesus' altar, and St. Thomas
altar 4   0
Received of Mr. Bell for the high altar *and two gates in the
churchyard* 6   8

Coates' Antiquities of Reading, 162.

Wigtoft Church, Lincolnshire, 1550.

Thes be yˢ receytt of yᵉ aforesayd Wyllm & Roger for yᵉ year. *s. d.*
Fryst of Gregory Wolmer, gent., for ye altar in our Lady
qwere 3   3
Item of John Wolgat for the altar in Nycholas qwere . 2   0
Item of Gorge Atkynson for the seyd (side) altar . . 10   0
Item of Kyrke of Boston for xxiii Stone of Leten* . . 8   4

The sale and seizure of altar candlesticks was general.
In the articles of visitation to be followed and observed according to *the king's majesty's injunctions and proceedings.*
1. That all parsons, vicars, and curates, omit in the reading of the injunctions, all such as make mention of the Popish mass, of chantries, of *candles upon the altar,* or any other such like thing; also no *minister is to set any light upon God's board at any time,*†—Art. 2. In Art. 9, " no man to maintain *lights, candles, altars,*" ‡ &c.

By these new arrangements, the chancel was rendered useless; for the table was ordered *not to stand altarways, but to be brought down into the body of the Church.* Thus the whole mystical arrangements of the ancient buildings were violated and destroyed, and screen, altar-steps, reredos, sedilia, sacrarium and sanctuary, were deprived at once of their original intention, and rendered useless; for the new form was indeed far more suited to the conventicle than to the glorious fabrics where it was performed, and which were mutilated, ruined, and defaced, to make them accord in any degree with the meagre novelties with which they were desecrated. On the revival of the ancient rites under Queen Mary, the preceding ravages were as far as possible repaired. In the archdeacon's " Visitation for London, 1554," the 5th article is as follows:—

" Whether there be in the church an high altar of stone, *consecrated and dedicated specially to sing or say mass upon;* and it is not meant any grave-stones taken up from the burial or other

---

* Leten, laten, the metal of which the candlesticks and other furniture of the altars was made.
+ There is no instance recorded in which the commissioners allowed candlesticks to remain in any church.
‡ Burnet's History of the Reformation.

unseemly place, and put up for an altar, but a meet and convenient stone as hath been accustomed in times past."—*Collins' Ecclesiastical Hist.* vol. ii. Col. p. 87.

In the Churchwardens' accounts of S. Mary's, Reading, 1558.

	s.	*d.*
Paide for the hallowing of the altars	13	0
Paide for a pynte of oyle	0	4
Paide for a pound and a half of franckeinsence .	0	11
Paide for v yards of cere cloth for the altars . .	2	8

Coates' Antiquities of Reading, p. 130.

In the parish annals of St. Pancras, Soper Lane, is a charge, anno 1555, Oct. 30, to *make up the altars* by November.

" Allhallows, Bread Street, 1554.

" The great stone which had been the cover of the high altar, was taken up from the body of the church, *where it had formed part of the pavement,* and was replaced for its original use."

These are merely a few random extracts, illustrative of the partial restoration of the English churches under the unfortunate Queen Mary. We shall now proceed to notice the destruction that again befel them after the accession of Elizabeth. This queen appeared in some respects rather favourably inclined towards the external splendour of the ancient faith ; and some of the ornaments that had been disused under Edward the Sixth, were retained in the Protestant service enacted under Elizabeth ; but the new clergy, and especially those she introduced into the sees of the old bishops, were Puritans at heart, and rather connived at these things from dread of the queen's displeasure, than adopted them from any veneration for ancient usages ; and, as we shall have occasion hereafter to show, they were soon abolished in practice, although they were theoretically held to the present day. The altars which the piety of the preceding reign had re-edified and consecrated, were soon ordered to be demolished, and in the act passed for that purpose, *the ordinary of the Church was constituted the overseer of this sacrilegious work.*

The period of Elizabeth is mentioned by some modern writers as the golden days of *Anglo-Catholic practices* ; but the following extracts will prove facts which are certainly incompatible with the existence of much Catholic feeling.

" Aug. 13, 1559, Skory, new Bishop of Hereford, preached at St. Paul's while the *visitation of the Church was in hand,* two days after the rood there, *with the altar, was pulled down.*"—*Strype's Annals,* vol. i. 134.

"St. Andrews, Holborn, 2d of Elizabeth.

"In the 1st and 2d year of her Majestie's reign, *all the altars and superstitious things* set up in Queen Marie's days, were now again (*to God's glory*) *pulled down.*"—*Nicholl, Lond. Red.* vol. ii. 187.

"2d of Elizabeth, St. Giles's Church, Reading.   s.   d.
For pulling down the awlters and rydding away of the rubbis   2   3

"St. Lawrence's Church, Reading, 1559.   .
For taking down the awlters and *layinge the stones* .   .   5   0
                              Coates' Antiquities of Reading.

"1559.   St. Margaret's Westminster.
Paid for taking down the table* over the high altars and
    taking down the holy water stock   1   0
1563.   Received for the altar table which was revived in the
    late Court of Augmentation, *defaced*   .   .   .   5   0

The altar itself escaped till 1570: for in that year we find the following item,—

For altering and *defacing* of the aulter stone and *laying down
    of the same*   1   4

Churchwardens' accounts of St. Helen's, Abingdon, A.D. 1559,
For taking down the altere   1   8
Payde for tymber and making the communion table .   .   6   0
For mending and paving the place where the alterre stoode .   2   8
                          Nichol's Illustration of Ancient Times.

Innumerable documents can be brought forward of the same kind as those now set forth, which prove the destruction of altars on the re-establishment of Protestantism under Elizabeth. Indeed the acts of parliament are themselves sufficient evidence of the fact; but as many persons are now endeavouring to affix the odium of this sacrilege on the Puritans during the great rebellion, we have selected corroborative testimony from parochial accounts, &c.

Strype, in his *Annals*, relates the queen was at first inclined to have such altars as had been demolished by the Protestant party in an irregular manner restored; but Cox, Sandys, Grindall, and others, drew up six reasons for the demolition, and eventually prevailed. These reasons are very similar to those urged in King Edward's days, and fully prove that the Anglican Church had abandoned all idea of the Eucharistic sacrifice. For in the fifth reason: "Furthermore, *an altar*

---

* The word table, as here used, signifies a tryptic, or folding picture of a centre and two leaves; these were frequently richly carved as well as painted.

hath *relation* to *sacrifice; so that of necessity, if we allow an altar, we must grant a sacrifice,*" &c.,—seeing the one was ordained for the other. No language can be clearer on this point, and it is evident that even the use of the word altar is scarcely allowable according to true Anglican principles.

The sixth reason is very important, as it shows that the modern recesses of the preaching houses of the day are in accordance with the spirit of Anglicanism. " Moreover, if the communion be ministered at an altar, the *godly prayers spoken by the minister cannot be heard of the people;*" and for this reason the table was brought down for the communion service, *where the clergyman might best be heard.* All the mystical reasons which instigated the erection of the ancient churches are here at once abolished; and this is one of the many evident facts, which should convince the good men who are so earnestly labouring for the revival of Catholic church architecture, that we must have the Catholic service revived, in the first place, before any real good can posssibly be accomplished,—unless this be done, difficulties arise at every step. The present communion is, after all, a sort of preaching service; it is not a solemn act of sacrifice, where the priest, in silence, within *the holy place,* is ministering for the people, according to the custom of even primitive antiquity;* but they are to assist, as at a sermon, by *listening* to the *clergyman.* This is pointedly assigned as a reason for demolishing the altars; because, if admitted at an altar, *the prayers spoken by the minister cannot be heard by the people.* Now it is very certain that the construction of the ancient deep chancels was entirely owing to the respect paid by our ancestors to the august mysteries celebrated within them. A deep chancel, under the present system is an absurdity; the very principles on which the Book of Common Prayer was framed are against it In fact, all idea of reverence ceased with its introduction, and chancels were filled with seats as early as 1578 (see parish accounts); and the reason assigned for enclosing the communion table with rails, was no other than *irreverent*

---

* The learned father Le Brun, in his "Liturgies de toutes les Eglises," 4 vols. 8vo., Paris, 1726, has gone at great length into the very important subject of the ancient manner of celebrating the sacred mysteries, and fully proves that from the earliest times the *communion was recited by the priest in silence.* This portion of the work is entitled " L'usage de réciter en silence une partie des prières de la messe, *dans toutes les Eglises* et *dans toutes les siècles.*" He cites the fathers, councils, and liturgies, in proof of this most important fact, which is an irresistible argument for the ancient construction of the churches, and also for the celebration of the sacred mysteries in the ancient language.

*people sitting upon it during service time.** The old churches are utterly unsuited for the present form of worship; and wherever we go, we find that immense sums have been expended on the ancient buildings, to ruin them and destroy all their beauty and propriety of arrangement; *abolish altars and sacrifice, and what can possibly become of a Christian church?* All the partitions, and dividing off of naves, filling up chancels with pews, cutting away screens, erection of galleries, are but consequences of the established system. These monstrosities followed as naturally in the wake of the Common Prayer Book, as chancels and crosses rose at the teaching of the ancient churchmen; and this will be perceived ere long by those who are making such strenuous exertions for the revival of ancient architecture. It may be urged, that the chancels were ordered to remain as in times past; true, but in this same order will be found a clause which deprived them at once of the very spirit of their existence: and we will ask, how long did the chancels remain as in time past? certainly not after a table was set at the lower end, and they were denuded of all their former glory. The walls and roofs might remain,—in some cases they remain now,—but *not as in times past:* and indeed it would be extremely difficult, if not impossible, to point out one instance where the chancel has been preserved with even decent respect; it is generally blocked up with pews, with backs to the east end, so as to face the pulpit; frequently it is one of the *common entrances into the church:* at Yarmouth the place of the table was occupied by *benches* on *evening lectures;* and along the Norfolk coast the *chancels of their truly glorious churches are, with very few exceptions, in ruins.* Again, the usual plan of converting the conventual churches into parochial ones, was to wall up the end of the nave, leave a few feet for the table, and either demolish the transepts and choir for materials, or leave them to decay. In cathedral churches the mob sit with their backs to the east, right up to the rails; and certainly, from the preceding note they did not pay greater respect to sanctuaries in Elizabeth's time, when Anglicanism was green and new, than they do at the present day.

---

* In the MS. visitation, preserved at St. Paul's, the following remark occurs, which shows the utter loss of all reverence for sacred places among the people of London in Elizabeth's reign, 1598: "In the upper quier where the common [communion] table dothe stande, there is met unreverente people *walking with their hatts on their heddes* commonly *all service tyme*, no man reproving them for yt."

But how could it be possible to preserve feelings of veneration among the people, when the altars were demolished, and the blessed sacrament itself, the soul of sanctity and veneration, expelled from the desecrated sanctuaries,—the relics of the ancient bishops and confessors turned out on a dunghill or consumed with fire,—and the portraiture of our blessed Redeemer and his saints hacked and mutilated? These fearful enormities have wrought such a debasement of feeling among the people of this land, that nothing but the almighty power of God can restore the blessing of reverence among them; and this cannot possibly be accomplished in any other manner than by the revival of the ancient faith; and the only misgiving we feel, respecting the labours of the present learned societies for the revival of church architecture, is the fact of their beginning at the wrong end, for unless the old faith and rites be restored, the deep chancels of antiquity would be no better than the other architectural masquerades of the day. An ancient chancel requires a consecrated altar, and a solemn sacrifice offered thereupon; it requires an assembly of the faithful, who do not come to *see and hear,* but to *assist in humble prayer at the celebration of the sacred mysteries,* and these require to be instructed in *the faith of the English Church, before her altars were overthrown, and her mysteries abolished, by Puritan bishops, and authorised blasphemers of sacred things;* truly there are other matters which require moulding to the good old fashion, besides blocks of stone and baulks of timber; and this must be evident to those who are labouring to preserve the departed glory of the sanctuary: not that we would by any means discourage their praiseworthy attempts, on the contrary, we hail them with thankfulness as the means of bringing men to reflect on glories they have abandoned and lost, and of comparing the wonderful achievements of our Catholic ancestors under the ennobling influence of the ancient faith, and the dismal results of the Protestant system of their latter times. A Catholic cathedral is no bad atmosphere wherein to imbibe a thorough detestation of Protestantism; for the contrast between the majesty of the building and the meagreness of the modern rites, appeal at once to the evidence of the senses:* and the study of ancient church architecture

---

* On the same principle a French cathedral of the present time is an excellent preventive against the revival of paganism; for here the abominations of modern design and trumpery stand forth in all their hideous inconsistency, by the side of the old Catholic work, which they dishonour by the intrusion.

is an admirable preparation for the old faith. One thing is certain, either the revival of true Christian churches, or the present service, must give way; for it is quite impossible for any man who abides in the Anglican Church, as she is at present constituted, to *build a Catholic Church and use it afterwards.* All that we have as yet seen attempted are wretched failures; every now and then we hear that a *real Catholic* church is going to be erected, and when completed, it has something of the shell of an old building, but no kernel; *it lacketh the one thing needful:* and there are certain inseparable arrangements which stamp Protestant on it at first sight: but if it were the very facsimile of Howden in all its glory,—when the consecration day arrived, and instead of the acolytes, and thurifer, and processional cross, and tapers, and copes, and mitres, and the holy chrism, and the pontifical with solemn antiphon, and the rich ferettum, with its saintly relics; the churchwardens are dressed in their best coats, and the charity children are drawn out, and a few Genevan gownmen appear as black as crows, and the bishop drives up with his lady;—the most resolute champion of Anglican rites, would relinquish his hopeless pretensions in despair.

But to return to communion tables. By the act of the first year of Elizabeth above-mentioned, which ordered the demolition of altars, the table was commanded to stand in the place where the altar stood, *except during the time of communion,* when it was to be brought down where the minister might be the more readily heard by the people; and after the communion, done from time tu time, the table to be placed where it stood before;—so that, inconsistently enough, by this arrangement, it was to occupy the proper position of an altar, *unless it was wanted for the purposes of communion.* But owing to the death of many of the old clergy, and the deprivation of many of the most learned and pious;—owing to their refusal to receive the new order that was attempted to be thrust upon them, there was not a sufficient number of learned men to supply the cures, and, to use Heylin's own words, the church was filled with an ignorant and illiterate clergy, hastily procured among *mechanics and others of the same class;* *

---

* John Rastel, in his answer to Jewel's challenge, thus addresses him, in p. 162 : " Whereas the Church of God, so well ordered with excellent men of living and godliness, is constrained to suffer coblers, weavers, tinkers, tanners, cordmakers, tapsters, fidlers, juglers, and others of the like profession, *not only to enter into disputes with her, but also to climb up* into pulpits, and to keep the place of priests and ministers ; or that any bagpipers, horsecoursers, gaolers,

while many were raised to great preferments, who, strongly attached *Genevan discipline*, had returned to England *much disaffected to episcopal government, and rites and ceremonies.* Accordingly, the *altar steps* were too Catholic for these new churchmen; and by 1561, we find that Parker was obliged to issue an injunction *against taking down altar steps*, and bringing the table into *the middle of the church*: by this new order, the communion table is commanded to stand in the place where the steps then were, or *had formerly stood*, which seemed to imply that it was not to be moved in time of communion. These injunctions could not have produced much effect, for, by the reign of Charles I, those clergy who attempted to administer the communion from the table so placed, were loudly denounced as favourers of Popery,—consequently the attempt must have been viewed as a restoration of an obsolete practice at that time.

The revival of this position of the table was undoubtedly owing to the celebrated and unfortunate Archbishop Laud; for, in the 19th of Charles I, we read in Rushworth's *Historical Collections*, that, in these times, the communion table *began to be placed altarwise in parochial churches*, after the manner of cathedrals.

And in vol. ii. p. 207, he gives some exceedingly curious particulars relative to a dispute between the parishioners of St. Gregory's Church, near St. Paul's, London, and the dean and chapter of that cathedral, who were the ordinaries therefore, and who had ordered the table to be removed up to the eastern end of the chancel, which gave great offence. A

---

aletasters, were admitted of old time into the clergy, without good and long trials of their conversations." The same author says in another place, " In the primitive Church, altars were allowed amongst Christians, upon which they offered the unbloody sacrifice of Christ's body ; yet your company [speaking to Jewel], to declare what followers they are of antiquity, do account it even one of the kinds of idolatry *if one keep an altar standing ;* and indeed you follow a certain antiquity, not of the Catholics, but of desperate heretics—the Donatists, who did break, rase, and remove the altar of God."

From the other charges urged by this writer against the Anglican Church, and which Peter Heylin says (in his "History," p. 347), " are too many *sad truths faithfully delivered*," we may gather that the following practices were by no means uncommon;—ministers using only their ordinary apparel while officiating in the church;—the processions in Rogation week retained merely for the purpose of keeping up the memory of the parish bounds, and not to move Almighty God by supplication for mercy;—the remains of the consecrated elements, after communion being taken by the clergyman, or parish-clerk, for their *own domestic use;*—that many of the new bishops refused to wear a white rochet, or to be distinguished from the laity by honest priests' apparel, and many other matters of a similar description.

similar case occurred about the same time between the parishioners and vicar of Grantham.

The history of the Anglican Church, in this eventful
period, must show the utter hopelessness of accomplishing
any restoration of ancient rites and reverence, excepting
through the *legitimate channel of real ecclesiastical authority.*
Of all Protestant churchmen,* Laud ventured the farthest in
his endeavours towards a partial restoration of ancient solemnity; yet never was there a more signal failure, and never
did a great man appear in a more pitiable and degrading
position than when he attempted a Protestant defence of
these proceedings, on his trial before the parliament. The
particulars of the charges brought against him are so curious,
and bear so strongly on passing events, that we have thought
it right to take some notice of them. One of the chief
articles was the ceremonies he used in the consecration of St.
Katharine, creed-church, London: the term consecration is
used by all the writers who have described the event, but as
St. Katharine was an old church, and had been only desecrated
by repairs, a reconciliation would have been a more correct
expression; but at all events, the ceremonies used by the
archbishop, if it be not using too irreverent a term, were a
mere burlesque of the ancient rites, and serve as a farther
proof of the necessity of adhering to authority and tradition
in these matters.

"First, as the bishop approached the west door of the church,
some that were prepared for it, cried with a loud voice, 'Open, open,
ye everlasting gates, that the King of Glory may come in;' and
presently the doors were opened; and the bishop, with some
doctors, and many principal men, went in, and immediately falling
upon his knees, with his eyes lifted up and his arms spread out, he
exclaimed, 'This place is holy! this ground is holy! in the name
of the Father, Son, and Holy Ghost, I pronounce it holy!' then he
took up some of the dust, and threw it up in the air several times
in his going up to the chancel. When the bishop approached near
the rail and communion table, he bowed several times, and retiring,
went round the church in procession, &c. After this the bishop
pronounced curses on those who should profane the holy place, and
blessings on those who should contribute to its support. Then
followed the sermon. This ended, as the bishop approached the
communion table, he made several lowly bowings, and coming up
to the side of the table where the bread and wine were covered, *he*

---

* When on the very scaffold, Laud declared he died as *good a Protestant as
any man in England.*

bowed seven times, and after the reading of many prayers, he came near the bread, and gently lifted up the corner of the napkin wherein the bread was laid, and when he beheld the bread, he laid it down again, stepped back, bowed three times towards it, then drew near again, and opened the napkin, and bowed as before. Then he laid his hand on the cup, which was full of wine, with a cover upon it, which he let go again, went back, bowed thrice towards it, then he came near again, and lifting up the cover of the cup, looked into it, and seeing the wine, retired back and bowed as before. Then he received the sacrament, and gave it to some principal men ; after which, with many prayers, the consecration ended."

Now throughout the whole of this ceremony, we cannot discover one act which was performed in accordance with any ancient ritual or pontifical ; the whole was an invention of the archbishop's, and filled with inconsistencies ; the antiphon, " Be ye opened," &c., said at doors, should only be used at the consecration of a new church ; for a reconciliation the bishop should commence the more appropriate antiphon, " Asperges me Domine," &c.

2. The bishop, immediately on entering, declared the place holy, pronouncing the supplicatory prayers to that effect after the benediction.

3. The matter of dust was a perfect novelty, blessed water being the matter used by the Church in benedictions; moreover, all matter used for such a purpose, requires to be first purified by prayer and exorcism, whereas the dust used by the archbishop was common dust from the pavement.

4. The altar of a church which is to be reconciled, should be utterly denuded of ornaments, while the communion table at St. Katharine's was prepared with the elements, cloths, &c.

5. The reverences made by the bishop to the mere elements previous to consecration, were utterly irregular, and even superstitious. But the defence made by the bishop when accused of these proceedings, was far poorer than the ceremonies themselves; he could not devise better arguments wherewith to defend the consecration of the church, than appeals to *Jewish practices* and *examples* of the *Mosaic Law,* which were very properly objected to by his adversaries as belonging to a dispensation which had passed away : he afterwards referred to the testimony of Eusebius, touching the consecration of the churches under Constantine, which was certainly more to the point. But when men are without the existing authority of the Church to appeal to, into what miser-

able evasions are they not driven! here was Laud, standing in the place of the lord primate of all England, appearing as successor to a race of prelates who had consecrated a long succession of churches and kings; and yet cut off from them by his protestations: he does not venture an appeal to the *ancient usages of the English Church*, but changes from Levitical ceremonies to Constantine, and then to the authority of Bishop Andrewes, an inferior ecclesiastic of course to the archbishop; and when pressed on the subject of images and sacred representations, appeals even to the heresiarch *Calvin*, to the no small exultation and triumph of his opponents, who at length overpowered and silenced the archbishop by quoting the homilies and common practices of the modern Anglican Church against him. This is indeed a most forcible example of the utter impossibility of any, but those who build on the rock of Peter, effecting any permanent good in the revival of ancient solemnity. Had the lot of Laud fallen in Catholic and better times, he would in all probability have proved himself a worthy successor of St. Austin; but influenced by his Protestant position, all that he accomplished in Church reform, was attained more after the manner of a temporal magistrate than with archiepiscopal authority. Accused afterwards of these very revivals, he endeavours to shelter himself under mean and evasive excuses; and when condemned (most unjustly) to die, he declares himself a *good Protestant*, and by that miserable admission forfeits all claim to martyrdom, and his decollation sinks at once to a mere state execution.

The other charges, which are detailed at length in Rushworth's *Historical Collections*, and other works, were substantially as follows:—

Setting up of pictures (stained glass) in the windows of his chapels at Lambeth and Croydon, bowing towards the table or altar, and using of copes at the sacrament. Now from the very fact of such charges being gravely preferred in the English Parliament against the archbishop, we may certainly infer, that the good practices complained of, *could not be very general* in the established Church at that period, 1643,

---

* We have, however, authorities to show that some copes were retained till the Rebellion, at the cathedral churches of old St. Paul's, Durham, Norwich, Peterborough, the abbey church of Westminster, the archiepiscopal chapels of Lambeth, Croydon, and the royal chapel of St. James's. At the three latter places they appear to have been introduced by the archbishop himself; and from the evidence of Laud, his predecessors must have allowed both the chapels at Lambeth and Croydon to fall into disgraceful decay; for he says, " that they lay so

10 Charles I; and we must moreover remember, that these charges were brought forward not on *professedly Puritan grounds*, but as *contrary to the religion as by law established;* and during the whole enquiry, the arguments made use of by the adversaries of the archbishop, were taken from the authorised rubrics, acts, &c., of the *modern Anglican Church:* but one of the most important facts to be gathered from these interesting proceedings, is the usual position occupied by the communion table, from the reign of Elizabeth to Charles the First. It was alleged, that the communion tables were *generally placed throughout the realm in the midst of the choir or chancel*, with the ENDS *east and west*, in which posture they generally *stood in all churches and chapels*, and in *Lambeth chapel itself for one;* since the *injunctions were published, till this innovating archbishop altered this their ancient position.*

It was therefore declared an innovation, and a Popish one too, tending to *remove the Lord's table as far as possible* from the *audience of the common people*, when the sacrament is celebrated at it.*

It does not appear that Laud ventured to set up any stone altar, or such an act would certainly not have been omitted in the charges alleged against him; his great offence seems to have consisted in placing the *communion table altarwise;* and the only authentic account of any attempt at the erection of a stone altar at this period, is to be found in the Grantham Controversy, under the title of *the holy table, name and thing.* It appears that the vicar had moved the communion table up to the eastern end of the church; and one Wheatly, an alderman of the place, commanded his officers to bring it *down again to its accustomed place in the church*, which was accomplished after some altercation, and even striking; upon this the vicar declared that he cared not what they did with their *old tressel*, for he would make him *an altar of stone at his own charge*, and fix it in the old altar place; the parishioners reply that he should set up *no dresser* of stone in the church; nor does it appear that he was ever able to accomplish his intention. All existing documents tend to prove, that *no altars*

---

nastily that he was ashamed to behold them." The period of Charles the First gave many indications of a reviving Catholic spirit; amongst other instances the parish church of St. Giles's, London, was glazed with stained glass, the parishioners combining and giving lights as in olden times.

* From this and other documents previously produced, it will be seen that *deep and reverend* chancels are utterly opposed to the principles and rubrics of the present Establishment.

whatever, old or new, were standing in the English churches at the commencement of the great Rebellion; and the Puritan faction must be entirely exonerated from the charge of altar demolishing, which has been preferred against them by those who are anxious to revive altars under the present system, and who would fain make it appear that dissenters, and not the establishment, were the altar-destroying party; but it will be seen from the evidence here adduced, that their position is quite untenable, and that those who are desirous of restoring *altars,* must first revive the rites and worship to which they belong.

On the ascendancy of the Puritan faction, most of those *altar steps* which *had not been previously demolished,* were ordered to be levelled, and the communion tables themselves in many instances were broken up and burnt. The principles of the Protestant Reformation were now fully developed, and all legal restraint being removed, the fanatics of the new opinions blazed forth in all their original fury, and scenes of Cranmerian violence were again enacted on those remains which had survived the first attack. These Reformers had, however, but little left whereon to expend their fury, except shattered windows, mutilated tombs, and bare walls; all the rich and costly decorations having perished in times of former outrage; and with the exception of some brass inscriptions, organ-pipes, and bells, they found little to satisfy their sacrilegious avarice. After the Restoration, the communion tables appear to have been generally set altarwise, as we now see them; and in order to accommodate this arrangement to the principles of the congregation *hearing the communion service,* in all churches built since that period we find the table is placed in a *mere recess,* a few feet deep, and railed off; and this is the correct arrangement for the present Anglican service;—it is certainly the antipodes of a *Catholic arrangement of a church;*—but the present service is not a Catholic service, nor was it composed by Catholics: it is of most Protestant origin, very Protestant in its character, and requires Protestant structures for its celebration; and it is as utterly impossible to square a Catholic building with the present rites, as to mingle oil and water. It is most delightful to see the feeling reviving in the Anglican Church for the sanctity and depth of chancels; and as a preliminary step to better things, it should receive all possible encouragement; but those who think merely to build chancels, without reviving the ancient faith, will be miserably deceived in their expectations; in these days there is certainly no fear of being hung or beheaded for such matters; but if the present revival of Catholic antiquity is suffered to proceed much farther, it will be seen that *either the Common Prayer or the ancient models must be abandoned.*

In tracing down the history of communion tables from the Restoration, we find them treated with little respect in any place, and usually with much indignity; in some churches they serve for the transaction of parish business, in others as the depository for the caps, cloaks, and wallets of the school children, who were *taught in the chancels as a spare portion of the church.* In those churches where communion service is celebrated only once a year, we not unfrequently find them moved altogether on one side, and generally rotten and disjointed, neglected and perishing;—perhaps a decayed and moth-eaten cover, whitened with the dung of birds, hangs in tattered fragments about it,—perhaps it is utterly bare.

A communion table serves a multitude of purposes: sometimes it forms a scaffold for the mason who is affixing a marble blister against the chancel arch; sometimes for the baptismal bason; sometimes for the parish register; occasionally as a rostrum for some vestry orator; and often as a seat for the cleaning functionaries to rest both themselves and implements upon. It would be tedious to lengthen this sad list of desecrations, which are common *even at the present time,* and universal but a few years since. A better spirit has at length arisen, and in many places the tables have been not only decently but well adorned, and what is far more important, the essential doctrine of the Eucharistic sacrifice is again put forth; but with what hope of ultimate success, at the present eventful crisis of events, it is impossible for human penetration to foresee.

SUMMARY OF THE ABOVE ACCOUNT.

1. All stone altars ordered to be demolished (as favouring the ancient idea of sacrifice) by Cranmer and his Protestant adherents, in 1550.

2. Stone altars revived under Queen Mary.

3. Demolished again by act of parliament under Elizabeth, 1559.

4. Communion tables, in lieu of altars, to stand in their place when not used; but during communion service to be moved down, for the purpose of enabling the minister to be better heard.

5. Ordered subsequently to remain at all times at the upper end of the chancel.

6. This order not observed. Communion tables left in the middle of the chancel, with the ends *east* and *west*, till partially changed'in the time of Archbishop Laud.

7. These changes made by the archbishop condemned as contrary to the spirit and ritual of the Anglican Church.

8. Tables after the Restoration placed altarwise.

9. Consequent shallow recesses, in lieu of chancels, introduced in all churches erected subsequent to that period.

10. Great irreverence exercised in general towards communion tables.

11. Partial revival of ancient reverence at the present time.

OF THE DESTRUCTION OF ROODS.

In every English Church, previous to the reign of Edward the Sixth, over the chancel screen stood a rood with the image of our blessed Redeemer crucified; and on either side, an image of his blessed mother and beloved disciple St. John. Of the propriety of such an edifying image in a Christian church, there can exist but little variety of opinion among men of Catholic mind; and the character of the reverence due from the faithful to so sacred a representation is admirably conveyed by the following lines, frequently inscribed over similar images on the continent:

> " Effigiem Christi dum transis pronus honora
> Sed non effigiem sed quem designat adora."

The antiquity of these roods is undoubtedly very great, and there is ample authority to prove that the image of our crucified Lord was sculptured on the rood previous to its introduction on the altar cross. Our present purpose is not however to enter on the history of the introduction of these sacred representations, but to describe their demolition. The first notice that we meet with in the annals of the Reformation respecting roods, is the account of the rood at Boxley, which was made to move with wires, and after being exposed to the people, was publicly burnt at Paul's Cross, on Sunday the 24th of February, 1538. If this was really meant as an imposture, the authors and abettors of it deserved burning far more than the image. But it seems very doubtful if it was, after all, any thing more than a figure used in the sacred plays, or mysteries as they were termed, and which were

frequently represented even in churches. Of the propriety
of these exhibitions it is not our purpose to treat; they
would be highly objectionable at the present time, but they
might have been productive of good at the time they were in
vogue, and it is difficult for us to judge accurately of the simplicity of those days. They can, however, be no longer a
subject of difference; as such representations have, since
the Council of Trent, been generally discontinued. But to
return to the rood of Boxley. What seems more confirma-
tory of the opinion that its machinery was not used for the
purpose of deception, is the fact that Henry was seeking
everywhere for occasions to justify in appearance the sacrilegious projects he meditated; it does also seem almost impossible that such a standing deception could be suffered to
exist in the diocese of an English bishop, and it is quite un-
accountable, that in the case of such a gross and blasphemous
imposture being discovered, the agents would escape unnoticed and unpunished; we have not, however, the least account of who they were, nor of their being even suspended
for the offence; and, taking all circumstances into consideration, there seems every reasonable probability of this far-
famed illustration of popish craft being nothing more than a
piece of ingenious but injudicious mechanism.

On the 17th of November, 1547, Heylin says: " the image
of Christ, best known by the name of the rood, together with
the images of Mary and John, and all other images in the
church of St. Paul, London, were taken down, as also in all
the other churches in London."

The parish accounts are exceedingly curious as details of
these devastations. The roodloft of All Hallows' Staining,
was pulled down in 1550, and the roodloft hangings fetched
twelve shillings. On the revival of the ancient faith under
Queen Mary, the parish churches were required to repair
these demolitions as speedily as possible. In the archdeacon's visitation for the diocese of London, printed by Collier
in his records for the Church History, p. 87, in the sixth
article is enquired, if there be a roodloft crucifix, as in times
past has been accustomed. The rood hangings of All Hallows' Staining, that were sold for twelve shillings, were re-
purchased in 1554 by the churchwardens at an advance of
two shillings; the new crucifix or rood cost 6*l.* 3*s.* The
parishioners of St. Pancras, Soper-lane, were enjoined in
October 1555 to make up the roodloft, with the rood, Mary
and John, of five feet long, by Candlemas.

K

St. Helen's Church, Abingdon, 1555.

	s.	d.
Payde for making the roode and peynting the same .	5	4
For making the roode lyghtes	10	6
Payed for peynting the roode, of Mary and John and the patron of the church*	6	0
To fasten the tabernacle where the patron of the church standeth	0	8

Among other expenses of St. Mary Hill, London, 1555, on the rood, Mary and John, the patroness, the *tabernacle of the patroness*, painting the patroness, and refreshing the tabernacle.

St. Giles, Reading, 1558.

Paid for making of a rode, with Mary and John, and for the making of the patron of our church . .	40	0

In 1560, being under Elizabeth, we find,

For pulling down these same images . . .	0	4
For *white liming the roode*	0	1

This was probably for the purpose of obliterating the painting on the loft; it shews that the whitewash bucket was very soon in vogue after the establishment of Anglicanism. Official injunctions were issued about this time for the total destruction of the roods with the images.

Strype relates in his *Annals*, that many crucifixes were brought by the people into Smithfield, and there broke to pieces and burnt; and he adds, "and this *was no more than were ordered by the Queen's visitors and her injunctions*, which were executed about Bartholomew tide, when in Paul's church-yard, as well as Smithfield, the roods (as they called the crosses) were burnt to ashes, and together with these in some places, *copes*, also *vestments*, *altar-cloaths*, *&c.*" Strype, at p. 135, gives an account of a sermon preached Nov. 5, 1559, at St. Botolph, Bishopsgate, at the *wedding of a priest to a priest's widow at Ware !!!* when one *West, a new doctor*, took occasion to speak freely and earnestly *against roodlofts*.

St. Margaret's, Westminster, 1559.

Item, paid to John Rial for his three days' work to take down the rood, Mary and John . . .	2	8
Item, for *cleaving* and *sawing* of the rood, Mary and John	1	0

This last item is another fearful illustration of the barbarous sacrilege of these times,—the image of our Saviour hacked and sawn to pieces !!

---

* The image of the saint in whose honour the church was dedicated, was usually placed in the roodlofts, and probably about the base of the cross.

Same year, St. Mary Hill, London.

For bringing down the images and other things to be burnt   1   0

St. Helen's, Abingdon, 1561. This parish, by the accounts, appears to have adhered to the ancient rites for some time; for there is an entry for candles for the Christmas morning at the mass under the above date, being the fourth of Elizabeth, and it was only this year the roodloft was destroyed.

To the somner for bringing the order for the roodloft   .   0   8

To the carpenters and others taking down the roodloft and
stopping the holes in the wall where the joices stood   .   15   8

To the peynter for writing the scripture where the roodloft stood   3   4

St. Andrew's, Holborn, first of Elizabeth: the rood, Mary and John, were this year burnt to ashes, by command of the commissioners. It is useless to pursue this sad catalogue of destruction any farther; sufficient testimony has been produced to shew that these *truly Anglo-Catholic* and edifying ornaments were not only removed and abolished owing to the establishment of Protestantism, but treated with the most barbarous indignity. The first rood set up in England, since the revival of Catholicism, was at the chapel of that zealous champion of the ancient faith of his country, Ambrose Lisle Phillipps, Esq.; and they are now commonly erected in the English Catholic Churches, with precisely the same ornaments and furniture as in times past.

SOME ACCOUNT OF OTHER DESTRUCTIONS THAT BEFEL THE ENGLISH CHURCHES, PRIOR TO THE GREAT REBELLION.

We do not pretend even to glance at the demolition of the great abbatial and conventual buildings, wherein perished many of the very finest monuments of ancient piety, but we purpose to confine our remarks to such cathedrals and parochial churches as were allowed to remain for religious worship. The inventory of plate, jewels, shrines, vestments, &c. which belonged to the church of St. Paul, London, prior to Henry VIII, occupies thirty folio pages of Dugdale's elaborate work on that cathedral. In the seventh year of Edward the Sixth, all the plate and ornaments suffered to remain in the church were as follows:

" Imp. chalices.

Item, 2 pair of basyns to bring the communion bread and offerings of the poor.

Item, a sylver pot to put the wine in for the communion table, weighing 40 oz.

Item, the written text of the Gospels and Epistles.

Item, a large canopie of tissew for the king's majesty when he cometh hither.

Item, a pall of black velvet to lay on the herse.

Item, a border of black sarcenet, with a fringe of black silk mixed with gold for the burial of noble persons.

Item, baudkins of divers sorts and colours, for garnishing the quire for the *king's coming*, and for the bishop's seat; as also at other times when the quire shall be apparelled *for the honour of the realm.**

Item, 8 cusheons.

Item, 30 albes to make surplices for the ministers and choristers.

Item, 24 old cusheons to kneel on.

Item, 7 cloaths of lynnen plain and diaper for the communion table.

Item, 5 towells.

Item, 2 hangings of tapestrie for the quire.

Item, a Turkey carpet for the communion table.

Item, a pastoral staff for the bishop."

And even these scanty ornaments were afterwards still farther reduced.

The inventory of the jewels and ornaments which anciently belonged to Lincoln minster, is given at length in Dugdale's *Monasticon Anglicanum.*

" Some idea of the surpassing beauty and richness of the ornaments may be formed from the fact of 2621 oz. of pure gold, 4285 oz. of silver, besides a great quantity of pearls and precious stones of immense value, being seized by the commissioners empowered by Henry VIII, for that purpose, June 11, 1540. Previous to that time, there were two shrines in the cathedral church : the one of pure gold, called St. Hugh's shrine, standing behind the high altar, near unto Dalison's tomb. The place is easily to be known by the irons yet fastened in paving stones there. The other, St. John of Dalderby : his shrine was of pure silver, standing in the south end of the great cross aisle, not far from the door where the gallery court is said to be kept."—*Dugdale.*

" In the seventh year of king Edward the Sixth, of all the ancient plate, there remained but three chalices, one pix, and an ampul."—*Ibid.*

" The church of St. Martin's, Ludgate, London, was richly furnished with plate, vestments, hangings, &c. Amongst other things, were seven chalices, which weighed 100 oz. ; a silver cross and

---

* The honour of festival days is not alluded to.

crucifix, 53 oz.; a thurible, silver, 31 oz.; the ship for ditto, 9 oz.; a chrismatory, 13 oz.; a berile, garnished with silver, containing the precious relics of saints; a tabernacle of silver, ornamented with the image of St. Martin; there were nine altar frontals of cloth of gold, embroidered, one with the twelve apostles; above the altar of our Lady was the coronation of the blessed Virgin, and in a second compartment the Salutation; before the rood were suspended hangings painted with the Nativity of our Lord, emblems of his passion, &c. with a multitude of other curious and rich ornaments, all sold or destroyed under Edward VI. In the year 1612, this church had but one chalice."—*Nicholson's Londinum Redivivum*, vol. iv. p. 363.

Dugdale says:—

"In the time of Edward VI, and beginning of Elizabeth, such pretenders were some to zeal for a thorough reformation in religion, that, under colour of pulling down those images here which had been superstitiously worshipped by the people (*as then was said*), the beautiful and costly portraitures of brass, fixed on several marbles in sundry churches of this realm, and so consequently in this escaping not the sacrilegious hands, were *torn away, and for a small matter sold to coppersmiths and tinkers*. Amongst the many that were at that time destroyed, those whose names I have here expressed, had their monumental stones and memorials here. Henry de Sandwich, Richard de Gravesend, Ralph de Baldok, Richard de Newport, Michael de Northburgh, Richard Clifford, Richard Hill, and Richard Fitzjames, as afterwards John Elmore, Richard Fletcher, and Richard Vaughan, all bishops of London; and many others."

Churchwarden's Accounts, St. Mary's, Reading, 1555.

"Item, Receyvid of John Saunders for 3 cwt. lacking 9 lb. of metal, that *was taken up of the greaves* and of old candlesticks, at 16s. the hundred . . . 46 2

"St. Andrew's, Holborn.

"1st, Edward the Sixth. 36s. were received from brass taken from the tombs.

"The tombs which formerly stood in the Grey Friars' church, Newgate-street (now Christ Church), and many of which were equal to the royal monuments at Westminster, were destroyed in 1545, by Sir Martin Bowes, mayor, who sold ten high tombs, and one hundred and forty grave stones, with brasses, for 50l."—*Stowe's Survey of London.*

To show the exact conformity of Protestant proceedings at different periods, we subjoin the following extracts from the churchwarden's accounts of Walberswick Church, 1644, about one century later.

April 8.   Paid for taking up the brasses of gravestones
   before the *officer* Dowson (William Dowsing) came .   1   0
Received for 40lbs. weight of brasses at $3\frac{1}{2}d$. a lb.   .   11   8
   " This system of plundering brasses was forbidden by proclama-
tion, in the second year of Elizabeth's reign ; but the prohibition
was little regarded."—*Weever's Funeral Monuments.*

It was by no means an uncommon practice for sextons to
sell brasses in Gough's time ; and it is most surprising that
any of these beautiful memorials of the departed faithful
have been found in the present time.

Church ornaments sold in the reign of Edward VI.

   " St. Mary Hill, London.
1547. Received of Jasper, the basket-maker, for $7\frac{1}{2}$ lbs.
   of alabaster* 0 17   6
For taking down the tabernacle over the vestry door,
   and other work 0 13   4
1549. Silver ornaments, sold at 5s. 8d. and 5s. 11d. per
   ounce, to the sum of   18   5   8
Charge for taking down the high altar .   .   .   1   2   6
   " Allhallow's, Staining.
1550. Two copes, 3 vestments, the cross banners, were
   sold by the churchwardens, for   .   .   . 6 13   4
Two copes and 7 vestments   4   0   0
Formerly belonging to the high altar of the said church.
   A silver gilt cross with images of the Blessed Virgin and St.
John, weighing 81 oz.
   Another cross of wood, plated with silver and gilt, with silver
images of our Lord, the B. Virgin, and St. John ; the five wounds of
our Lord were five rubies ; in the base a crystal, with the holy
name ; a pax of mother-of-pearl, set in silver, another of silver gilt,
with the crucifixion, two thuribles, $63\frac{1}{2}$ oz., 4 chalices from 12 to
8 oz.
   In 1551, three of these chalices were sold at 6s. an ounce.
1609. The church possessed but one chalice and patin.

   " Allhallow's, London-wall.
   The high altar was adorned with the following rich ornaments :
a cross of silver, parcel gilt, weighing 93 oz. ; two chalices, 12 oz.
each, and a third, $9\frac{1}{2}$ oz. ; a chrismatory, $20\frac{1}{2}$ oz. ; a cross to bear the
blessed sacrament ; a pax, 6 oz. ; a do. with three images of sylver ;
a pontifical of St. Thomas of Canterbury, clossed in silver ; a bone
of St. Davy, clossed in silver ; a chalice, 8 oz.
   In 1572, this church did not possess a single article of silver ;
the sacramental *vessels were all pewter.*

---

* This was evidently alabaster carving and imagery.

" St. Mary's, Reading.

1551. Sold to Sir Thomas Wynsore, knight, two altar cloaths of Tyshewe, and two white vestments for deken and subdeken.

Item, sold to two men of London the sute of crymsyn velvett, with eleven copes of the same, a cope of blewe velvet ; with a vestyment and one dekyng, the best canopy, four corporis cases (burses) with four old copes, and an old vestyment, 14*l.* 13*s.* 4*d.*

Item, the church plate sold as followeth ; that ys to saye, the whyte and the parcel gylte, for 5*s.* 4*d.* the unnce, the gilt 6*s.* the unnce

Item, two belles sold weighing 38 cwt. 4 lb. at 30*s.* the cwt.

Item, ten foder of lead* sold at 6*l.* 16*s.* 8*d.* the foder.

" St. Lawrence, Reading, 1546.

1546. Received for certain plate sold, that is to witt a bason weying 23 oz. ; a censer weying 30 oz. ; a pomannder,† 3½ oz. ; a shippe weying 9½ oz. ; a chrismatorie, weying 22 oz. ; the silver uppon ye boks (probably the holy gospels), weyhing 13 oz. ; an old crosse, weying 3¼ oz.—at 4*s.* 9*d.* the once.

" Ditto, 1549.

Received for the remaining church plate, 48*l.* 18*s.*

Paid to the carpenters for taking down the images and tabernacles, xii*d.*

Paid to N. Bell, mayor (*of that was made of a chalice*), for paving in the streets, 54*s.* 4*d.*

Paid and delivered by N. Bell, by N. Nicholas, upon the *two chalices sold by him, towards the pavinge of the strets,* 53*s.*

---

* The following letter, from Richard Bellycys to Cromwell, time of Henry the Eighth, is a curious illustration of the lead-stripping period: "Pleasyth your good lordshipp to be advertysed I have taken down all the lead of *Jervase*, and made itt in pecys of half foders, which lead amounteth to the numbre of eighteen score and five foders, with thirty-four foders which were there before. And the said lead cannot be conveit nor carryed until the next sombre, for the wayes in that contre are so foule and deepe that no carrage can passe in wynter. *And as concerning the raising and taking doune the house,* if it be your lordship's pleasure I am minded to let it stand to the spring of the yere, by reason of the days are now so short it would be double charge to do it now. And as *concerning the selling of the bells,* I cannot sell them above fifteen shillings the hundredth, wherein I would gladly know your lordship's pleasure, whether I should sell them after that price or send them up to London; and if they be sent up surely the carriage wolbe costly frome that place to the water: and as for Byrdlington I have done nothing there as yet, but sparethe it to Marche next, because the days are now so shorte ; and *from such tyme as I begyn I trust shortly to dispatche it in such fashion that when all is finished I trust that your lordshipp shall think I have bene no evyll howsbound in all such things as your lordshipp had appointed me to doo.* And thus the *Holy Ghost ever preserve your lordshipp* in honour [blasphemous scoundrel] ; at York, the 14th day of November, by your most bounden beadsman, RICHARD BELLYCYS.—*Hist. of Bridlington, Rev. M. Pricket.*

† A silver vessel like an apple, filled with warm water, for the priest to warm his fingers during excessive cold, to prevent accidents in handling the chalice.

" St. Giles, Reading, 1549.

For stones of the crosse sold, 2s. (this was probably the cross in the churchyard.)

1560, 2d of Elizabeth.

Paid for pulling down of images, 4d.

" St. Margaret's, Westminster.

1552. .Paid for a *a recreation for the quest,* on the 12th of July, when they came to view the inventory of the church goods 6 8

Paid to Mr. Curat and Nicholas Poole, for making the book of the church goods to be *presented to the king's commissioners,* and the pains they took about it . . 10 0

The result of this quest was the sale and destruction of the ornaments.

The hideous boarding, with the writing, at the back of the communion table, in place of the ancient reredos, is mentioned as early as 1547.

Paid for 2 waynscotte boards, for the high altar . . 1 0
Paid for wryghtyng of the scriptures upon the same boards* 5 0

1547. The churchwardens sold images and altar curtains to the amount of 3l. 6s. 8d.

1549. There appears to have been a tumultuous assembly to hear Lattymer deliver one of his irreverent discourses; for we find, "paid to William Curlewe, for *mending of diverse pews,*† when Dr. Lattymer did preach." The congregation must have been very disorderly, for the seats at that time were not ¾-deal, but 3-inch oak.

In *Neale's Parish Churches,* a most curious inventory is given of the plate, vestments, and ornaments, which belonged to Long Melford church, Suffolk; the whole of which were removed, sold, plundered, or destroyed, in the reign of Edward VI. Geneva psalm books are frequently mentioned.

" Abingdon, 1573. Payde for a quire of paper to make 4 bokes of Geneva Salmes, 4d."

Whitewashing was introduced very early, probably for the purpose of effacing the ancient paintings and ornaments on the walls.

---

* " Walberswick church, 1596. Payd unto the paynter for writing of the ten commandments and *making of the queen's arms,* 14s. 4d.

† The open seats were called pews, but regular Protestant pews, lined with baize, &c., were erected in this church as early as 1611. " Item, paid to Goodwyfe Wells, for salt to *destroy the fleas in the churchwarden's pew,* 6d.

" Great Wigston, Leicestershire, 1591.

Paid John West, for whitewashing the church . 1 18 10

" St. Mary's Reading, 1551.

Paid for the whyte liming of the church . . 0 14 8

The following letter, sent by the commissioners under Queen Elizabeth to the Dean and Chapter of Bristol, will fully account for the horrible mutilation of the altar screens in that church, and many reredoses of exquisite beauty that were defaced at the same time.

" After our hartie commendacyons. Whereas we are credibly informed, that there are divers tabernacles for images, as well in the fronture of the roodloft of the cathedral church of Bristol, as also in the frontures, back, and ends of the wall where the communion table standeth ; forasmuch as the same church should be a light and good example to th-ole city and dioc. we have thought good to direct these our desires unto you, and to require you to *cause the sade tabernacles to be defaced and hewn down,* and afterwards a *playne wall* with *mortar, plaster, or otherwise,* and some scriptures to be written in the places, and namely, that upon the wall where the communion table doth usually stand, the *table of the commandments painted in large characters* with convenient speed ; and further according to the orders lately set forthe by virtue of the queene's majesty's commission for causes ecclesiastical, at the cost and charges of the said church, whereof we require you not to faile, and so we bid you farewell. From London, the 21st of December, 1561."

Here then is an injunction issued by the glorious Queen Bess and her *Anglo-Catholic* officers, which cannot be distinguished, either in terms or intentions, from the orders issued by William Dowsing or any other Puritan of Cromwell's time. It is certain that we owe the preservation of such glorious monuments as have yet escaped, more to inadvertency, or sheer weariness of destruction, than to any better cause : such injunctions as these, if carried out, would have demolished the screens of Winchester and St. Alban's, equally with those of Bristol ; for *niches* and *tabernacles* are things here described: the images had been defaced or removed under Edward the Sixth, but even the screens themselves were far too popish for the new system. At that period all the dignitaries of the Church *were confirmed Puritans ;* * there was no other class of ecclesiastics to be found who would con-

---

* Amongst these we cannot omit to notice Dean Wittingham, who was appointed by Elizabeth to that noble church of Durham : where holy Cuthbert and venerable Bede once lay gloriously enshrined ; and this wretched Puritan soon completed the havoc and destruction commenced under Henry, and carried on by Edward's commissioners. Heylin says that this man had been at

sent to the innovations, and after the deprivation of the old Catholic ecclesiastics, their offices must have been supplied by the Genevan men, or left altogether vacant. Afterwards a better spirit sprang up, of which Laud, Andrewes, Hooker and others are instances; but they could effect little : and Protestantism, combined with the universal decay of Catholic art and feelings throughout the world, has so altered the English churches, that the very best are but lamentable wrecks of their former glory.*

the head of the Francfort schismatics ; and, while dean of Durham, actually advised and aided the infamous John Knox, in setting up Presbyterianism in Scotland.   Certain is it that this noble abbey, which but few years previous to his time was inferior to none either in richness or solemnity, became a perfect wreck under his control ; and he scrupled not to deface the tombs of the bishops, and even to apply the sacred ornaments to profane uses.

" The priors buried in the centry garth had each one a tombstone, either of marble or freestone, which *Dean Wittingham caused to be pulled down and taken away ; and broke and defaced all such stones as had any pictures of brass, or other imagery work, or chalices,* wrought upon them ; and *the rest he took away and employed them to his own use, in making a wash-house at the end of the centry garth for his laundresses ! ! !*

" Within the abbey church were two marble holy-water stones, bossed with hollow bosses, on the outsides thereof curiously wrought.   These were taken away by *Dean Wittingham, and removed into his kitchen, and employed to profane uses :* they stood there during his life ; his servants steeped their beef and saltfish in them.   Moreover, *Mrs. Wittingham,* after her husband's, the dean's death, took away the lesser holy-water stone, and had it set in the kitchen in her own house.   She likewise carried from the centry garth several gravestones of *blue marble, and other tombstones that lay upon priors and monks, which she built in her own house,* in the Bailey."—*Sanderson's Antiquities of Durham Abbey.*

The same destructions were carrying on, at the same time, in other cathedrals, by Puritan deans and bishops, with the aid of their wives and servants. The immense body of evidence that can be collected on these matters, would prove the Puritans of latter times to be only faint imitators of their originals. Every bishop of the Establishment was *de facto* an altar demolisher and Iconoclast ; even stained glass was quite contrary to the real spirit of Anglicanism. In a word, under the system as established the cathedrals were useless, the parochial churches inconvenient, and the ancient ornaments incongruous.

* No doubt England deserved this scourge ; she had become unworthy of the blessings she enjoyed ; and this dreadful chastisement may have been given in mercy ; but whatever ulterior good may be eventually brought about by this awful convulsion, surely it is most inconsistent for any man to *defend the instruments of this searching visitation,* and to glory in their humiliation and decay. As well might they extol the cruel Jews who nailed our Lord upon the cross, or the traitor Judas who betrayed him, because such things were suffered by God to be.   Let sounder views of persons and events arise, and party altercations cease ; there is but little cause to boast.   The Catholics lacked faith and zeal, betrayed their trust, renounced their spiritual obedience, and even participated in Church plunder ; Protestants were sacrilegious, fanatical, and filled with blasphemous heresies ; they were the firebrands of God's wrath, to lay waste the vineyard ; and those who defend either them or the system, or who would palliate their offences, are guilty of defending sin, and participate in their guilt.   And, on the other hand, let no Catholic suppose that the *cause* of this tribulation came from *without.*   Here, in England, in Catholic England,

From these lamentable chronicles some correct idea may be formed of the desecrated state of England's churches after the great schism of the sixteenth century. Truly does it seem that the words of Jeremiah in his Lamentations had come to pass in this unhappy land: "Viæ Sion lugent eo *quod non sint qui veniant ad solemnitatem*, omnes portæ ejus destructæ, *sacerdotes ejus gementes, virgines ejus squalidœ*, et ipsa oppressa amaritudine." Again, "Quomodo obscuratum est aurum, mutatus est color optimus, *dispersi sunt lapides Sanctuarii* in capite omnium platearum;" and yet this dark and dismal period of sacrilege, of infidelity, and irreverence, is strangely distinguished as *Anglo-Catholic*, by men who are professionally engaged in building up the walls of Sion. The misapplication of the term *Anglo-Catholic* at the present time is truly surprising, and by gross inconsistency it is used *exclusively* to signify times and events *essentially Protestant*. While the almost Puritan service of the last three centuries, composed under the immediate superintendence of *foreign heretics*, with all its meagreness, departure from antiquity, and inconsistency, is denominated Anglo-Catholic, the ancient rites of the *English Church, which she held in common with the rest of Christendom*, are termed Romish, and not unfrequently this expression is actually applied to the very liturgies and ceremonies compiled by the old English bishops, and which were in a manner peculiar to this country. The modern English service is *very Genevan*, but the ancient English liturgy, although approved and sanctioned by the holy see, was *not Roman*. Gregory of ever-blessed memory, commanded St. Austin to adopt such rites and customs as he found practised in the churches of those countries through which he passed on his journey to England, as might tend to the increase of edification; and to introduce them in the English Church: and we may reason-

---

was a stronghold preparing for that monster heresy, in the hearts of those who should have stood like bulwarks against his approach. The spirit of luxury, the spirit of indifference, the spirit of the world, were extending among all ranks. Sacraments were neglected, apparel was extravagant, mortifications were rare, humility had fled,—pride and paganism were spreading fast. And when novelties and infidelities arose, they found a soil prepared to nurture them, in a land where in better days they would have been withered in a moment: for Protestantism *cannot plant itself, much less take root, in a truly Catholic atmosphere*. England's Church had degenerated, and it fell; and when Protestants can be brought to view the things in which they now glory, as so many vials of God's wrath, and when Catholics discern the true causes of this sad decay, and, burning with zeal and faith, stand forth with ancient devotion and fervour, despising the world and all things but God and His holy Church, and shine as lights before their fellow-men, then may we hope indeed for the blessings of unity and peace.

ably conclude, that ours was a very perfect ritual. At the time when Calvin undertook to revise and alter the English Liturgy, was it not filled with commemorations of those saintly prelates and kings, who had shone as lights of faith in this once truly glorious land? and had not a canonised bishop of England composed so holy and approved an office, that in the missals and rituals it is termed "ad usum *insignis et præclare* ecclesiæ Sarum?" was not God worshipped with marvellous solemnity in the old English Church? and indeed, was there any portion of Christendom to be compared with it, for the multitude and glory of its pious monuments and religious buildings? and while many of them were erecting, Rome was a perfect desert. Yet in face of all these facts, we continually hear of "Romish altars," "Romish roods," "Romish ceremonies," "built by the old Romans," "a Roman priest" (probably a rector with a chasuble and chalice, who never was out of England in his life), "Romish bishops," "Romish superstitions," and the like; and men have been so deluded with these ideas, that they have brought themselves to hate the Church of their country and of their fathers as *foreign*, and to embrace and cherish *really foreign novelties* as English. But it is to be remembered, that although these ancient glories were by God's blessing brought to the highest perfection in this land, we did not possess or hold them as *Englishmen*, but as *Catholics;* our country was as indeed a bright gem, but it was only one jewel in the crown of the Catholic Church. And although in the days of Faith we were permitted to excel most other nations in the majesty of our rites, it was by virtue of our communion and holy obedience to Christ's vicar, the Bishop of Rome, successor to the Prince of Apostles. Once severed from his authority, cathedrals, abbeys, cloisters, altars, shrines, bishops, priests, lands, and privileges, availed nothing, —they passed away at a breath. Their glory was as a dream, and their place knew them no more: the source of life was severed, and they were dried up and withered away. And let those who think by mere arch or pinnacle to revive solemnities and retrieve the past, read the awful lesson of England's punishment written with iron hand on every glorious pile. When courtier bishops and trembling priests first signed the fatal act of schism, that separated England from the mother church of Rome, their possessions were ample, their pastures were green, their buildings were spacious, lofty, and beauteous, the furniture of the altars was all-glorious, the majesty of the temples was unimpaired, and the Church of England seemed like a fabric, so strong, so venerable, and so mighty, that it could not be shaken. And for a few days' length it looked the same, and the matins were sung, the mass was solemnized, the procession winded through the aisles, and tapers burnt round the shrines, and in the foolishness of their hearts the people said, what need have we of any pope? but a dark speck soon appeared on the horizon, and a whirlwind of destruction arose, and the foundations of this vast fabric were undermined, and the choirs ceased to echo with the sound of praise, and soon they were roofless; and the lights of the sanctuary were extinguished, and costly jewels and gold were no longer to be seen; and the relics of saints were scattered, and the treasures of the Church were pillaged, and her authority became a name, and the altars of God were overthrown, and the image of Christ was defaced, and strange ministers stood in the temple of God and mocked the olden solemnity. And although three hundred years have passed away, and men have somewhat of a *taste* for the things that their *fathers revered*, and axes and hammers are laid by, and restorations are in hand, yet when we stand beneath the vaulted roof of Catholic antiquity, and view the motley group that sit in old churchmen's stalls to hear some anthem sung, while the stripped and mutilated sanctuary is abandoned and forlorn, filled up with benches of the meanest sort, we must in sorrow feel that the anger of God is not withdrawn, that His hand is still heavy on us; and we may in truth exclaim—"Patres nostri peccaverunt et non sunt; et nos iniquitates eorum portavimus:" nor can we hope to see England freed from the curse that has fallen on her for her ancient offences, till the cause which provoked it is removed. Let those, then, who would build up the sanctuary of God, first prostrate themselves in humility before the tribunal of Christ upon earth, and then, under holy obedience, and in the true spirit of England's ancient Churchmen, turn to the re-edification of those material temples which heresy has defaced and destroyed; but the present system is too rotten and decayed to work upon; and patching up Protestantism with copes and candles, would be no better than whitening a sepulchre: for choirs, chancels, altars, and roods, have no part with modern Liturgies and Calvinised rubrics; either the things or the system must be abandoned: the glories of pointed architecture, if viewed *distinct from their Catholic origin, and as symbols of the true and ancient faith* lose at once their greatest claim on our veneration; and far better would it be to see the churches left ruined as they are than revived as a mere disguise for Protestantism. We hail the present feelings of admiration for Anglo-Catholic antiquity only as a probable means of eventually restoring the faith, and not as an abstract question of art or taste; but let us hope that God in his mercy has stirred up these sentiments in the breasts of our separated countrymen, for the accomplishment of some great end; for if they fail in working them out to a right conclusion, the cause is hopeless indeed; the English Catholics are too reduced and degenerated to accomplish any revival on the great scale of antiquity; moreover, the fervour of their ancestors does not shine by any means conspicuous among them; and what has been already accomplished under these unfavourable circumstances is little short of miraculous; and by showing what a *few* out of a *remnant* who work on the old foundation can achieve, should serve as an encouragement to others, who have greater means and equal desire, but want the authority. In a word, the will is on one side, the power on the other; once united, a few years would restore centuries of decay. One thing, however, seems certain, that we must shortly prepare for some wonderful change to be worked, either on the side of God or of Satan; for those who are really animated with Catholic feeling will never remain satisfied with the mere shadow of antiquity; and Protestants and infidels clamour loudly against the trifling return to mere decorum that has already been accomplished in certain places.

The *via media* is rapidly narrowing on those who tread that dangerous and deceptive road; it will soon be utterly impracticable. Two paths will then present themselves for choice: *this* returns to England's Church, with her priests, her altars, her sanctuaries, and her ancient solemnity, communion with Christendom, and part with her glorious saints and martyrs of old; *that*, on to the conventicle, with its preaching throne and galleries, the divisions of dissent, and portion with heresiarchs and blasphemers. The hour is at hand when ambiguous expressions and subtle evasions will no longer shelter or conceal. Men must stand forth the avowed champions of Catholic truth or Protestant error; and blessed indeed will they be who, at the hour of trial, fail not, but, counting all loss as gain in the cause of Christ, apply themselves to the holy work of England's conversion, like blessed Austin of old, strengthened and supported by that rock of Peter which cannot be moved, and against whom the world and Satan shall never prevail.

FINIS.

For EU product safety concerns, contact us at Calle de José Abascal, 56–1°,
28003 Madrid, Spain or eugpsr@cambridge.org.

www.ingramcontent.com/pod-product-compliance
Ingram Content Group UK Ltd.
Pitfield, Milton Keynes, MK11 3LW, UK
UKHW010336140625
459647UK00010B/634